Early Childhood Education and the Student Empowerment Program

Early Childhood Education and the Student Empowerment Program

Mario C. Barbiere and Jane C. Wiatr

ROWMAN & LITTLEFIELD
Lanham • Boulder • New York • London

Published by Rowman & Littlefield
An imprint of The Rowman & Littlefield Publishing Group, Inc.
4501 Forbes Boulevard, Suite 200, Lanham, Maryland 20706
www.rowman.com

6 Tinworth Street, London SE11 5AL, United Kingdom

Copyright © 2020 by Mario C. Barbiere and Jane C. Wiatr

All rights reserved. No part of this book may be reproduced in any form or by any electronic or mechanical means, including information storage and retrieval systems, without written permission from the publisher, except by a reviewer who may quote passages in a review.

British Library Cataloguing in Publication Information Available

Library of Congress Cataloging-in-Publication Data

ISBN 9781475856057 (cloth)
ISBN 9781475856064 (pbk.)
ISBN 9781475856071 (electronic)

Dedication

This book is warmly dedicated to all of the children whose experiences led me to want to write a book; to my husband, Walter, for his kind listening ear and untiring support; and to all of my family, then and now, including all of the Jacks, who are so special in my life. It is dedicated to all those who said "I am so proud of you" for sharing your knowledge with others.

It is for Doc for cowriting this book with me and understanding early childhood education and realizing that two brains are better than one.

A special remembrance dedication is written with heartfelt memories to one of the best Kean University professors. Dr. Michael E. Knight is remembered for teaching me to be the best teacher I could be and for instilling in me a philosophy that states "children are to be handled with tender loving care." Mike's demeanor was nothing short of an epitome of a true early childhood educator, providing his knowledge and experiences, supporting and mentoring, and allowing his scholars to experience and learn by doing. His memory will shine within me and with you as it is passed from person to person through this early childhood book.

It is time to begin the journey together.

—Jane

I dedicate this book to my twin brother, Ray, whom I will miss; my brother, Charlie; my mother and father, who insisted I go to college; my four sons, Jim, Chris, Mike, and Matt, who gave life meaning; and to Kermie, who believed in me and made me who I am today. Your love, kindness, compassion, and smile are forever.

This book is dedicated to all educators who go to school each day and bring hope to their scholars. We never want to take away hope, as that to me is the only thing a child has.

—Mario

Contents

Preface		ix
Introduction		xi
1	*The Student Empowerment Program* and the Early Childhood Learning Brain	1
2	The Nature of the Learner and the Early Childhood Learning Brain	23
3	The Classroom Environment and the Early Childhood Learning Brain	35
4	Play and Exploration and the Early Childhood Learning Brain	49
5	Lesson Design and the Early Childhood Learning Brain	61
6	Assessments and Rubrics and the Early Childhood Learning Brain	79
7	Technology and the Early Childhood Learning Brain	93
8	Tying It All Together	113
Index		125
About the Authors		133

Preface

Early Childhood Education and the Student Empowerment Program is a hands-on, must-have book for teachers, support staff, administrators, and parents who want to advance their knowledge about early childhood education, promote positive student behavior, and teach student self-regulation. The book is designed to help the reader easily implement an exemplary early childhood program that focuses on positive discipline and student self-regulation, whether it is a public or private school setting.

If you are a new teacher, an experienced teacher, a member of the support staff, a day-care provider, or a parent, this book will help you implement positive student behavior through the implementation of the *Early Childhood Education and the Student Empowerment Program*. It will provide information about the nature of the learner, so you can construct lessons that promote student engagement. The authors will discuss the developmental stages of the early learner's brain and discuss how the brain is actively ready to learn in the early childhood years and how it is important to work to build and secure a foundation for later learning.

Early Childhood Education and the Student Empowerment Program instructs the reader in a step-by-step process with the development of the 5Rs—responsibility, reflection, rules, regulation, and rubrics—which results in the students' taking charge of their own learning. The onus is on the students to learn how to become introspective, so they can learn to evaluate their behavior while playing and working in the social, emotional, and cognitive domains.

With the onset of universal preschool in the United States, we understand that addressing the needs of educators is imperative. We have firsthand knowledge, which we will present to you in a simple format, one that you will easily be able to employ from the very first days of school.

Dr. Barbiere (Doc) is a retired teacher, vice principal, principal, assistant superintendent, superintendent of school, and school turnaround specialist, who served as the executive director for the Comprehensive and Support Interventions Division of the State of New Jersey. Mrs. Wiatr (Jane) is a retired early childhood educator, an antibullying specialist, and an intervention and referral service and 504 chairperson. Together, through the True North Achievement Project, Jane and Doc present workshops on education and have gained a real sense of what is necessary for success by staying abreast of the research in the field. You may be surprised by our nontraditional methods, but we can assure you that both authors have tried and tested our strategies from the prekindergarten to the college classroom.

Enjoy your journey, as the first step was opening the cover. The rest will flow, and you will be well on your way to your new commitment as a change agent and student advocate.

Introduction

The Student Empowerment Program is a whole-child approach to brain-based learning in early childhood education. The book and its contents are denoted as an informative and practical guide to teaching for both new and seasoned teachers, administrators, support staff, and parents. The book spotlights *The Student Empowerment Program* and the 5Rs and is the foundation for a positive climate and culture in the early childhood classroom. It is the architecture you need to build a solid foundation for learning and the information you need to move your students toward taking the onus for their own learning, becoming self-dependent learners and not teacher-dependent ones.

Universal preschool is the new initiative of the US government, which seeks to expand education to include the four-year-old early childhood learner. Dr. Barbiere and Jane Wiatr have discovered through their field experiences that many professionals are requesting guidance now that they are faced with a new set of students and a new set of standards. This initiative, although new to many, is one that Doc and Jane have experienced in their years of teaching, as both educators and parents and with which they have practical experience. The authors have assisted many professionals in learning how to implement the skills, strategies, and techniques you will become familiar with in this book, over many years.

Administrators are questioning how to incorporate the four-year-old into the school so that, in a year, the transition to kindergarten is smooth, curriculum is consistent, and positive behaviors are in place by the time the child enters the next grade. The teacher is faced with the need for classroom management that works, as the social, emotional, and cognitive domains of the four-year-old are much different from those of a kindergartener and the parents will want to support the school, but are without a plan or a toolbox to do so.

The Student Empowerment Program addresses all of these needs and more. This book specializes in the prekindergarten, kindergarten, and early elementary school classroom and prepares all stakeholders for teaching methods that work, behavior methods that correct without negative actions, and an action plan for parents and teachers to use together in support of each other.

The Student Empowerment Program can be used when conventional methods of discipline are failing. It is a behavior modification program for a whole school, or it may be used for individual children at home by their parents. Any educator who wants to make a positive change and become enabled to teach more and discipline less will appreciate the simplicity of our style in this step-by-step handbook. Parents who require assistance with positive behavior modification strategies will find our process an easy one to implement.

The eight chapters are quite explanatory and detailed specifically to address the nature of the learner in many areas of the curriculum, from play and exploration to technology to rubric and assessments. The nature of the learner is a term used throughout the book and one that describes how the student learns in a developmentally appropriate way and how the teacher learns to teach to different learning styles. Our focus is on the learner. We have covered the gamut of what all educators need to know to become masters in their field of education. The reader will find research-based strategies, examples of methodology, lesson plans, reflective exercises, regulation practices, rubrics, and much, much more.

The chapters are in sequential order beginning with an explanation of the program itself. From here, the model expands upon itself and scaffolds the learning for the reader. It builds slowly and allows you time to incorporate the practical application for each chapter. You will be given time to reflect upon your own teaching, and there are areas where you can note changes you will make or have made within the context of this handbook.

Finally, the authors can be reached for further questions by contacting them by email at True North Achievement Project or tnapcoaching.com.

CHAPTER 1: *THE STUDENT EMPOWERMENT PROGRAM* AND THE EARLY CHILDHOOD LEARNING BRAIN

The focus of *The Student Empowerment Program* is to facilitate the students' becoming self-dependent and not teacher-dependent learners, so that learning can and will take place. We walk the teacher through the 5Rs process without putting undue stress on the already busy schedule a teacher faces in the world of teaching. We will guide the reader into a positive change resulting in the students' taking the onus for their own learning.

CHAPTER 2: THE NATURE OF THE LEARNER AND THE EARLY CHILDHOOD LEARNING BRAIN

When defining the nature of the learner, we think of the cognitive, social, and emotional characteristics of the student. These characteristics are what regulate learning. The reflection of and by the learner and the teacher, as well as the feedback provided by both and how it is implemented by both toward the students' success, is what defines the nature of the learner.

CHAPTER 3: THE CLASSROOM ENVIRONMENT AND THE EARLY CHILDHOOD LEARNING BRAIN

The classroom environment begins with the warm smile from the teacher and staff members. Acceptance, tolerance, diversity, integrity, honesty, and all of their counterparts make up the part of the classroom that is not physical, like chairs and tables. We must establish an environment that is open and accepting from the first day of school, so our students can learn together in a positive environment that is safe and secure. The classroom is transformed in such a way that creativity and critical thinking are steadily increased.

CHAPTER 4: PLAY AND EXPLORATION AND THE EARLY CHILDHOOD LEARNING BRAIN

Play is the work of children. It is perhaps the most effective way for them to learn life skills and to find out what they like or dislike. In this chapter, we discuss the types of play and how children's developmental levels influence their play and play responses. We compare theorists such as Piaget, Montessori, Brazelton, and Vygotsky to understand the importance of exploration in play. We define the teacher's role as facilitator and instruct how not to step over the "helping" boundary, but deliver help through open-ended questioning techniques.

CHAPTER 5: LESSON DESIGN AND THE EARLY CHILDHOOD LEARNING BRAIN

In this chapter, we will address the changes in the formats of lesson designs over the years. We will also take a close look at how to design a lesson with the nature of the learner in mind. We will discuss the Core Curriculum Content Standards, as well as the early childhood learning standards, which are critical components to daily lessons. In addition, we will discover the project-based learning approach in early childhood education, as well as higher education, and we will discuss the attributes of lesson design and lesson delivery.

CHAPTER 6: ASSESSMENTS AND RUBRICS AND THE EARLY CHILDHOOD LEARNING BRAIN

In early childhood education, would you think that a standardized bubble test would be applicable for the students? We would think not, as it is obvious that you cannot test children on their creativity, leadership qualities, small- and large-group play, language use, and demonstration of understanding. A prekindergarten classroom, as well as an upper elementary classroom, should implement the use of behavior and academic rubrics. These rubrics allow the children to reflect upon their own learning, as well as acting as a valuable reflection tool. Reflection is the key to regulation, and, through these two processes, the children will gain feedback needed to monitor their own progress and make changes.

CHAPTER 7: TECHNOLOGY AND THE EARLY CHILDHOOD LEARNING BRAIN

As teachers, we want to establish the learning environment so that technology enhances learning and student metacognition. We want to marry technology and lesson design so that they work together and technology remains as an alternative way of delivering a lesson. A classroom emulates a video-gaming scenario for the student by establishing rules, protocols, and clear positive behaviors for appropriate actions.

CHAPTER 8: TYING IT ALL TOGETHER

This chapter is one that collaborates all that is taught throughout our book. All of the instruction is now set into motion using our techniques while maintaining balance in the environment and applying our techniques to more structured academia in later early childhood grades. The chapter walks you through each phase of the 5Rs so that you may begin implementing the program on the very first day of school and, from that moment forward, continue to build upon your new knowledge to create an environment conducive to learning and one where the children are self-regulated and in which the students challenge their own learning to a higher level of success.

Chapter One

The Student Empowerment Program and the Early Childhood Learning Brain

All learning is emotional. Start with a safe and positive emotional environment and learning will take place.

—Dr. Mario C. Barbiere

FOCUS OF THE CHAPTER

The focus of this chapter is our brain-researched project, titled *The Student Empowerment Program*. Our objective is to facilitate the student to become a self-dependent and not a teacher-dependent learner, so that learning can and will take place. We will walk you through the procedure without putting undue stress on the already busy schedule you, as a teacher, face each and every day. We will guide you into a positive change, resulting in your students' taking the onus for their own learning. We have gathered strategies and techniques that have been used with students and proven to be successful.

In this chapter, we will address what to do when the "learners" need support in their cognitive, social, or behavioral (emotional) domains. We learn at different rates and in different ways, so we must understand the nature of the learner in order to accomplish student goals and for the student to become adept and successful at learning. We want to facilitate self-regulation and self-control in our students, so that an observable increase in learning will occur.

FOCUS QUESTIONS FOR THE CHAPTER

1. What do I do when the student has a social or behavioral issue that results in a disruption in the classroom?
2. How can I stop the negative student behavior and not lose control over the rest of the class and/or situation?
3. What types of behavior modifications should I use to create a classroom that reflects a positive culture?
4. What is *The Student Empowerment Program*?

5. What are the 5Rs, and how do I implement them with my students?
6. Should the 5Rs be implemented schoolwide or only in a single classroom?

INTRODUCTION

This chapter will discuss a new program called *The Student Empowerment Program*.

It has been in practice for many years and is the brainchild of Dr. Mario Barbiere and Jane Wiatr. It provides teachers with the opportunity to teach more and discipline less and provides the students with rubrics, so that they may embrace the onus for their own learning.

Teacher-reported problems that need to be addressed for positive classroom management:

1. Students do not follow the rules even though they are posted on the wall.
2. Meltdowns are frequent among some children and interrupt the lesson.
3. Children do not seem to understand respect of self and others.
4. There is a lack of student attention, focus, and engagement.
5. Students lack responsibility for homework, classwork, and group work completion.
6. Students lack a sense of self, as if they are in a different place and time, and, when called upon to perform, they are confused or "missing in action."
7. There are a lot of "hyper" kids.
8. Work in class in not of high caliber even though we know the student can do better.

IN THE BEGINNING

The Student Empowerment Program is a brain-based program, and when all stakeholders are committed to it, it has proven to be effective in changing the culture of the classroom, as well as preventing unwanted negative behaviors. It provides the teacher the opportunity to focus on the lesson implementation and deal less with corrective behavioral actions. It is a stand-alone program and can be implemented in one or more classrooms. It can be delivered as a schoolwide option to include all staff and personnel. It can be correlated with any curricula, including those whose concentration is on self-regulation, as this program will complete the cycle of learning by adding rubrics and mindfulness.

SETTING THE STAGE: BEGIN WITH ESTABLISHING A CLASSROOM CLIMATE (STAGE 1 OF THE LEARNER'S BRAIN MODEL: THE PLANNING STAGE)

When constructing the classroom climate, the teacher begins by setting the prevailing mood, aligns adult and child attitudes, sets high standards of respect and character education values, and models tone of voice and body language. These traits will encompass the feeling that dictates the classroom atmosphere conducive to learning the entire year. A negative classroom climate can make the environment feel hostile, chaotic, and out of control. A positive classroom climate feels safe, respectful, welcoming, and supportive of student learning. The brain reacts to an unsafe environment in one of three ways: fear, flight, or fight. Any and all of the three ways are *not* conducive to learning. Information is processed in the hippocampus area of the brain, and, if the brain feels threatened, the autonomic nervous system takes over, and the body reacts. The brain needs a safe environment and needs *not* to feel threatened for learning to occur.

As the teacher enters into the implementation of *The Student Empowerment Program*, she begins to set a positive tone to correct unwanted behaviors. The teacher can begin to do this by building relationships with the students through greetings and a smile when they enter the classroom. Once the students are in their classroom, the teacher should learn the students' names and something important about them as soon as possible.

Next, the teacher will formulate rules with the class for procedures to work and the classroom to be safe and secure. The teacher will continue to build a rapport with the students while introducing smooth transitions and expectations in and out of the coming days. The teacher will post examples of expected behavior in picture form, as well as written, and model appropriate behavior while she is teaching.

Use open-ended questioning, as opposed to questions that develop a yes or no answer. Open-ended questions help to create a communication and a relationship between teacher and student. As teachers develop relationships with students, they can link students with students and connect with families and community members.

TEACHER PRESENCE

When we discuss the teacher's presence we think about the teacher and her *being* in the classroom. This includes her emotional state of mind and her readiness to teach, plus her abilities to meet the needs of her students. Teachers serve as facilitators of children's growth and development, and they need to reflect upon the value of the good that is in each student. Teachers need to draw out and share that good so that it emanates as one of the facets of the climate of the classroom. It is the teachers' responsibility to be positive role models for their students. Responsibility plays a huge part in the atmosphere of the classroom, as respect develops out of responsibility to self and others through reflection. Setting a positive classroom culture that promotes student self-regulation in a positive classroom can be done using *The Student Empowerment Program.*

THE STUDENT EMPOWERMENT PROGRAM

The Student Empowerment Program creates a positive response when it is delivered. The instruction is heightened, and learning is the best when everyone takes a few minutes to reflect, relax, and regulate their minds and bodies. Mindfulness is defined as the awareness and attention one gives to his or her mind to concentrate. Take a moment to intentionally focus on something positive to slow your heart rate, relax your mind and body, and align your neurological system, as well as your spirit.

Mindfulness does not require a lot of effort. Build time into your daily schedule, and implement the strategies and techniques listed in this chapter. The sooner you implement mindfulness in the class, the faster the students will learn what their bodies feel like and begin the self-regulation process. An out-of-control body is hard to manage, whereas a regulated body is easy to manage. A mindful body of a student who is regulated is also ready to learn.

These strategies are good ones to begin, ones that have proven successful and are the most appropriate for early childhood learners.

MINDFULNESS ACTIVITY

Try this exercise.

1. Preread numbers 1–7.
2. Take a deep breath, and rate from 1–5 (with 1 being the lowest rating and 5 the highest) how you are feeling right now. Write down your rating.

Proceed:

1. Sit up straight in your chair.
2. Roll your neck twice in a circle if you can.

3. Fold your hands in your lap.
4. Breathe deeply twice, in through the nose and out through the mouth.
5. Count to 10 slowly and methodically.
6. Imagine you are standing at the water's edge, with the warm sun and bright blue water surrounding you (mindful imagery).
7. Open your eyes and reflect upon how you feel.

HOW DO MINDFULNESS AND IMAGERY SUPPORT CHILDREN'S LEARNING?

Mindfulness implementation in the classroom can change behaviors and patterns of thinking and restart the child's body and mind toward a new positive one on the spot. The child can switch it off and on to something more productive and less negative with the ability to implement this strategy. This is a huge step in managing the classroom.

Engaging children in breathing and movement activities helps them become more aware of their bodies and the sensations within their bodies. They become focused on themselves and their environment. This process teaches them how to use their breath to focus their attention and calm themselves. The goal is for the children to learn techniques that they can employ later when they need help *regulating* their emotions or behaviors. Remember, the process requires practice, as one cannot do it once and feel the full impact.

Here is a sample of practices. These will help to create a classroom climate that is reflective, respectful, regulated, and positive.

1. Ask your students to lie on their back or sit on a chair. Set a timer for 30 seconds. Ask them to listen, and then discuss what they heard. When 30 seconds has ended, ask whether anyone had difficulty focusing on just the sounds around them or whether their mind wandered to something else. Request that they just listen to the sounds (you may say "I need you to listen to only the sounds around you"). Now, set the timer for one minute, and ask them to listen to the sounds around them. They may hear indoor or outdoor sounds, their own breathing, talking in the hallway, footsteps, and more. When the minute is over, immediately ask them how they feel, not what they heard. Then, ask them to draw or write about what they heard, or discuss it with a partner in a pair share.
2. Breathing techniques
   a. Back-to-back breathing: Partners are back-to-back and breathing with each other.

b. Tummy breathing: Lay down on the floor with a stuffed animal on your belly, and watch the animal rise and fall as you breathe deeply.
c. Elephant breathing: Clasp hands together. As you breathe in, raise your arms over your head, with hands still clasped, and then as you breathe out, lower them in front of your body/how the trunk of an elephant swings.
d. Bubble breathing: Hold an imaginary bubble wand, and blow through it. Imagine it has happy feelings inside.
e. Balloon breathing: Place your hands on the side of your mouth and blow out. Expand your hands slowly to the sides as the imaginary balloon gets larger.
f. Shoulder roll breathing: Raise and lower your shoulders as you breathe in and out.
g. Bumblebee breathing: Place each pointer finger on the outside flap of both ears, and push to close the ears off from sound. Next, hum and pretend to be a bumblebee. Hum in slow mantra-type sounds.
h. Take five breathing: Stretch your hand outward to see five fingers in front of you. With the other hand, start the roller-coaster ride from thumb to pinky and back again while breathing slowly and methodically. (https://childhood101.com/fun-breathing-exercises-for-kids/)

3. Emotional Freedom Technique (EFT): EFT uses the body's meridians, which are aligned with acupressure techniques. It is another type of mindfulness process in which the person doing it uses self-talk and breathing techniques while massaging or tapping areas of the body.

The areas of the body are listed below. Next to the area, we have placed suggestions regarding what your students may say while massaging or tapping. Language should be changed to fit the circumstance and or developmental level of the child.

- Karate chop: Tap edge of hand with other edge of hand a few times. Breathe.
- Over eyebrow: Say "I am thinking of something."
- Side of the eye: Say "I am having trouble concentrating."
- Under eye: Say "So many things to think about."
- Under the nose: Say "It's OK to feel this way."
- Chin: Say "I know I am a great boy (girl)."
- Collar bone: Say "It's OK to focus right now."
- Armpit (side of ribcage): Say "I am an important member of this class."
- Crown of head: Say "I am great." (Tapping 2018)

When we think about breathing and mindful moments from a neurological point of view with a connection to the brain, we see that when our emotional brain is stressed, our breath is rapid, as is our heart rate. When this happens during a school lesson, little or no learning will take place. This "magic" connected breath sends a message to our amygdala, and our amygdala begins to calm. This message is sent to the frontal cortex, and learning can now take place in a regulated and controlled way.

USING IMAGERY IN LESSONS

As you learn to use imagery in your classroom lessons, you will be able to support your students throughout the universe, on trips of their imagination. Think about this statement: "Throughout the universe, on trips of their imagination." Did you see the imagery in your mind's eye? If you answered yes, you are beginning to discover what imagery is in the mind. When you think about something, you formulate thoughts. These thoughts can be collaborated with pictures or visuals in your own mind, thereby making the whole scene much more real or fantasy-like.

By using towels as magic carpets or clouds or even spaceships you will change the feeling of your guided imaginary. The students will want to participate, so feel free to whisper open-ended questions and include your crew as they participate in the journey.

You are actually covering your language arts literacy goals when you tell the story and include the comprehension objectives. Be creative with the children and build stories that have sense and meaning to them. If you know there is a conflict in the classroom between students, use this time to "fly" to PS Land. The children learn that PS Land is where *problems are solved*.

You can certainly use this time to teach empathy, compassion, and tolerance toward others without mentioning the actual problem that ensued in the classroom. Your imaginary lessons will increase in the students' development and successful learning will take place. PS Land is a conflict-resolution tool that leads to learning how to cope, tolerate, be fair and equal, and solve problems among peers. It is a great stress reliever.

REFLECTION

The process of reflection involves linking a current experience to previous learnings (a process called scaffolding). The process involves drawing cognitive and emotional information from several sources: visual, auditory, kinesthetic, and tactile. To reflect, one must act upon and process the information and synthesize and evaluate the data. In the end, reflecting also means applying what was learned to contexts beyond the original situations. What did the experience teach me, and how will I apply it in future experiences?

As a teacher, you will want to look at yourself (personal reflection) and teach the children how to view themselves in that "mirror." You should observe and evaluate what you see, think, and feel by using internal feelings and the five senses. This evaluation process will lead to concrete decision making and the next course of action. This course of action is the precursor to regulation, and regulation leads to self-dependent learning.

The Value of Reflection

Improvement in learning is cited when children can reflect, predict, and question their own learning. Conflict resolution, problem solving, communication, critical thinking, and higher-order brain skills are a result of reflection.

Costa and Kallick (2008) list the stages of reflection in chart A (table 1.1). This will enable the teacher to better understand the developmental levels of reflection and make clear what expectations should be set for our students. Chart A notes the teacher making reflections in the early grades by prompting the younger learners to begin to build reflections on their own. In the upper grades, reflection is shown by student input, and finally in grades 3 and 4, the teacher prompts again for more intense and deeper reflection. Chart B (table 1.2) lists how these strategies can be applied to the classroom.

Table 1.1. Chart A: Stages of Reflection (Stage 1 of Learner's Brain Model: The Planning Stage)

Kindergarten	Teacher describes what is drawn.
	Teacher focuses on drawing.
	Teacher comments on realism of the picture.
	Teacher shows interest (what the student really loves).
	Teacher mentions use of color.
	Teacher mentions use of letters.
	Teacher pays attention to what letters spell.
1st Grade	Teacher focuses on conventions.
	Teacher wants paper to have a neat appearance.
	Teacher talks about what is liked in drawing.
2nd Grade	Student focuses on details.
	Student focuses on colors.
	Student shows development of an idea.
	Student relates to content of story (how student feels about the content of what was written).
3rd–5th Grades	Teacher responds in depth on student dictation.
	Student starts to write by himself.

Table 1.2. Chart B: Classroom Application

Kindergarten	Rubrics, journaling, coloring, guided imagery, brainstorming, artwork and music expression, questioning, self-talk, counting to 10, conflict resolution strategies
1st Grade	Student interviews, sentence journals—student uses a given sentence to think/dissect a quote, hypothesize, predictions, write a letter, finish the story with your own ending
2nd Grade	Teacher encourages students to do double-entry journals if . . . then . . . , provides sentence starters, encourages students to use goal-setting plans of action, maintains student work folders and portfolios
3rd–5th Grades	Teacher uses group discussions, essays, feedback communication journals, retrospective research papers, peer mediation, peer-to-peer mentoring

Reflection Tips

Reflection should be ongoing. Make reflection an ongoing part of the program day. Set aside a set time when children gather in a small group to share what they have done. Eventually, it will be part of their classroom routine, and they will look forward to these meetings.

Use feelings charts, mood charts, feelings thermometers, learning pictures, thoughts of the day, and activities that help children discuss their favorite or least favorite ideas. The use of visuals will enable children to share their emotions in a nonverbal manner. Visuals address the visual learner, as well as the noncommunicative special needs child and the ELL student.

Ask open-ended questions. Open-ended questions allow for discussion, as opposed to closed (yes/no questions). Once the question is posed, follow-up questions can be asked to promote reflection. As with planning questions, they should be specifically designed to draw upon previous learning and connect it with new learning.

Observe and take anecdotal records. As a teacher, you need to observe and assess daily activities. When you listen and reflect upon how and what the child is doing, you can expand language by asking more questions or by adding commentary or activities to the learning.

Write down what the children say. Write what you hear the child say during playtime, work time, rest time, snack time, and throughout the day (anecdotal records). At the end of the day, practice this fun reflection exercise:

> The name of this exercise is Ask Mr. Hootie Owl. Using the quotes that you scribed from the children during the day, you will pick five quotes and ask the children whether they remembered "WHO SAID IT." You will find that children remember who played with whom and who played with what, and others

remember that it was their quote. The anecdotal records are used for formal assessments too.

Accept conflicting viewpoints and interpretations. Not everyone has the same opinion, and we want to value and respect other people's opinions, so the students feel that the environment is "safe." Children perceive things differently from adults. Listen first and ask questions second. You may start by saying, "I am listening to you and I would like to hear you tell me what you know." Remain neutral in the discussion.

Understand the difference between reporting and tattling. Reporting is when you tell an adult to help someone who needs help. *Tattling* is when you tell an adult because you want to see someone get in trouble. Simply stated, *reporting is helping someone who is in trouble; tattling is getting someone in trouble.*

Comment on what you see the children doing as they play. Explaining a situation can help the dual-language learner, the special needs or nonverbal child, and a "normally" developing student, but you will not want to intrude into their moments of discovery. The teacher will want to facilitate without crushing the creativity and expression of the child.

Wait time. You will also want to allow time *after asking the questions* so that the child has time to think (reflect) critically about the answer. Wait time is important. Allow up to 10 seconds for processing/reflection and answering before prompting for an answer.

Think about how much you direct the child. The most successful teachers and the most positive classrooms are the ones in which the facilitator allows for child-directed activities, and this includes problem solving. This means that the teacher states exactly what she observes during conflict resolution issues. It may be warranted to allow them to work out the problem, with the teacher silent, but very close by observing the steps the children take to resolve their issue.

There are many teachers who want to give direct instruction and will interrupt the play to correct the problem or change the course of the play, but, if the teacher comments only on what she sees the child doing well, the child will learn what is correct and what is acceptable and will repeat the desired behavior at another time. It's OK to choose to say nothing.

The teacher may need to go a step further and state something positive that's not quite there, so that she can lead the child into better actions or language. For example, if the child is running during walking time, you may say, "Sophie, your feet are slowing down to a walk. You are really showing me great control, and you are following our classroom rules." Set up expectations through feedback.

Help children connect their plans and activities with their reflections. Often, a child will start with one plan for playtime and then switch gears to another plan. It is important to discuss what is being offered at the centers before dismissing the children to the free playtime. If the child changes her course of play during playtime, it is acceptable, as long as the teacher is aware of the process. Change creates independence and critical thinking. It is positive and shows the beginning of self-reflection.

Encourage children to carry over their activities to the next day. Theorist Maria Montessori was a strong proponent of continual learning. Through her work with the five senses and the hands-on learning technique, the child was able to connect to real-world experiences. It didn't matter how long it took the child to complete the goal of the learning activity. What was important to Dr. Montessori was that life skills were developed, so that the child could aspire to be a meaningful member of society.

Many teachers make a game of cleaning up at the end of the day, but many children don't want to clean up in the middle of working. They really want to continue their plan, creativity, and discovery during the next free playtime. This style of teaching lends itself beautifully to reflection. Think about what you did yesterday, plan for today, and complete the action today or tomorrow.

SELF-CONTROL VERSUS SELF-REGULATION

Self-control is inhibiting (preventing) strong impulses. For example, a person may love to eat chocolate. Self-control would be to resist eating three pieces of chocolate when you usually eat two. Self-control is *not* continuing to eat the chocolate by inhibiting the strong impulses because you said you are on a diet and you are not eating it at all.

Self-regulation is reducing the frequency and intensity of strong impulses by managing stress load and recovery. As for self-regulation, one will decide to limit the chocolate to one piece and not to continually eat the chocolate. It is self-regulation that makes self-control possible or in many cases unnecessary. The reason lies deep inside the brain.

If you look inside the brain of a child who is highly aroused, you will see a limbic system lit up in bright shades of red. The limbic system, which is the source of strong emotions and impulses, is in control and overriding other parts of the brain. Hence, that is why we say "all learning is emotional." Calm down or make the situation safe and learning will occur. The brain is always in a survival mode, as survival is a strong instinct. The task is to move from the survival mode (limbic system dictating action) to the learning mode (the prefrontal area making decisions). As stated earlier, the shift from "survival brain" to "learning brain" is critical for learning.

SELF-REGULATION PROCESS

The *first step* in the self-regulation process is called foreknowledge. Foreknowledge enables the student to know what she will need to become regulated. Prior to the foreknowledge stage, the teacher ensures that the student understands SRL (self-regulated learning) strategies, so the student can employ these strategies when a teacher is not available. In the early childhood years, the teacher should use the strategies that we have covered thus far in this chapter— breathing, imagery, and reflective strategies and techniques— as the foundation for the self-regulation process. The atmosphere has been created so that regulation can fall into place.

Self-talk is an essential component during this transition. This encourages instant self-reflection, self-talk from the student, breathing, and finally regulation.

SELF-TALK AND SELF-REGULATION: AN EXAMPLE

Two students are fighting over the same truck. One "wins" the truck, and the other has an "angry moment."

Angry Student: "I want that truck!" The child *does not* immediately employ the self-regulation strategy, as he is *in a moment of fight or flight/emotional response*, not regulation, and at his young age he still needs guidance to regulate. The older, more practiced child has the self-regulation skills and stopping the action is easier. In addition, the teacher will need to reflect to evaluate why the younger child did not begin the process. What has she possibly missed in the instruction?

Teacher: "I hear your loud voice and I see your red face." The teacher is just noticing "for" the child what he should be feeling and hearing in himself, which is that the temperature of his face is rising and his voice is escalating.

Teacher: "What can you do to help yourself feel better right now?" The teacher takes it one step at a time. The teacher does not address the problem, as that is what has escalated the unregulated behavior. The teacher begins to guide the child into the reflection by reminding the child about his understanding of the strategies she has taught him to use when he feels angry. The teacher is also reminding the child that she trusts him to gain control and that she will help him learn to regulate and help him problem solve. The teacher is not going away, and the child knows and feels this natural response. He is beginning to recognize his internal feelings.

Teacher: "I see you are breathing normally now. You did a great job counting. I could hear you count from 1–10 in a controlled way. I see your head is up and that you are thinking about how to control your body. Nice job; you are making good changes. You do not have that red face or loud voice any longer. You have your normal school face, and you are using an inside voice." The teacher has built a foundation of success and defused the issue for the child. She is teaching the child to self-regulate, even though she may not be seeing it happen "exactly" as she would expect or desire.

Student: Mumbling under his breath, repeating to himself (self-talk). The student is breathing in through his nose and out through his mouth. He is beginning to calm due to the breathing mechanism and the neurological system. This is why *breathing* is a natural word choice, as it is an involuntary action. There is always a success with it.

Student: Breathing, and counting in a low voice and sitting down on the floor.

Teacher: The teacher is aware of student, but no overreaction is seen, nor is she speaking with the student at the moment.

Student: The student stands up and comes over to the teacher and says "I don't want to play with her."

Teacher: "I hear what you are saying. I see that you have controlled yourself. Your face is pink again and your voice is normal again. I hear what you are saying (repeats this as she is letting the student know that she will address it and she thinks what he says is valuable) and I saw how upset you were a moment ago." (Teacher repeats what she said earlier to reinforce the self-control rule).

Teacher: "How do we figure out this problem? Do you have an idea?"

Narrative: Teacher and student discuss problem and solution together. Until the student was regulating his behavior, the teacher remained "out of the problem." She kept her eyes on the child to make sure he was safe and secure and added very few words, only enough to prime the child to begin the independent action of regulation. When the child was feeling less stressed, he came over to the teacher, who was waiting for him. She did not give any negative feedback to the child like "snap out of it." The use of questioning after the "meltdown" happened next. The problem remains, and the child is not ready to figure it out for himself. So the teacher will address it by prompting him to answer.

Teacher: "Do you remember when we used the timer (in the problematic past) last time this happened? Do you remember how it helped each of the kids with the problem like yours share the toy they were troubled over?"

(*Troubled* is a perfect word to use, as it is not "in trouble," but the situation was problematic, not the child.)

The other scenario that may have occurred is that the child regulated and then, instead of coming to the teacher, would have gone to the student with the truck and suggested that they share based on the use of the classroom timer for toy sharing, a solution strategy that has been discussed and in place since September. In this case, the teacher would keep a keen eye on the articulation and body language of both children and watch the problem solve itself. The teacher would intervene only if help was needed or to keep the timer on task.

If the child just gives up and retreats as some children may do, the teacher will want to intervene to teach sharing and cooperation. The self-control will be apparent, but the lack of "energy" given to the problem solve is an issue that needs to be addressed, so that the child learns how to solve conflicts. This scenario took time, but it is time well spent now so less time is spent later.

For self-regulation to occur, self-regulation learning strategies must be taught by the teachers, and the earlier the better. Teachers should model the process whenever possible and explain to the students what they are doing so students understand that they are learning a process. The teacher can say "If I am having a problem doing my work, I can turn to a friend for help. I can use resources in the room." Or the teacher can say "This is what you should do if I want to improve your grade on an assignment. First, check your grade, and then look at the rubric to see what you can do to improve that grade."

The *second step* is to construct a classroom environment that promotes self-regulation. The self-regulated classroom provides rubrics, exemplars, and a meaningful environment and encourages the use of journals, work folders, and portfolios to construct a learning environment where students can learn and apply self-regulation.

The *third step* is for the teacher to tell the students she will be monitoring their progress, but she wants them to self-monitor their own progress too. "I will teach you strategies, but we will also be using rubrics (and exemplars), so feel free to get out of your seat to check them. While doing your home learning, continue to monitor and gauge your own learning." Monitoring and regulation is the next stage, and the child has to know what strategies to employ (table 1.3).

Table 1.3. Comparison of Self-Regulation versus Self-Control

Self-Regulation	Self-Control
Self-regulation makes self-control possible by reducing the frequency and intensity of strong impulses, managing stress load and recovery. Self-regulation focuses on the "thinking brain," executive function area to the brain or the prefrontal area.	Self-control is about inhibiting strong impulses. It involves the center of the brain, the hippocampus or limbic area.
Self-regulation is planning and modulating your action to avert problems. "Planning before the fact." It is important to remember that self-regulation strategies must be taught and it is better to start at a young age.	When thinking about self, think that it is a mental activity. It is like stepping on the brakes to stop. If you don't step on the brakes early enough, you will plan next time to do it earlier. Act early or plan later.
Self-regulation involves actions using the executive "learning brain."	Self-control involves reactions and occurs in the "survival brain" (cerebellum or lower brain), which is in the center of the brain.
Self-regulation occurs in the prefrontal cortex, the home of our rational, reflective self.	Think of self-control in terms of "cognitive competencies," i.e., things like reappraisal, self-distraction, self-soothing, or weighing up the consequences of an action. When a reaction to an event occurs in the limbic area, the brain goes into a survival mode.
Actions are suppressed in the prefrontal cortex area when the brain is in "survival mode" since the brain is concerned about survival, as it is the utmost important task.	Self-control is not likened to deciding to speed, but more like slowing down to prevent an accident. It's really more a case of averting an accident and putting on the brakes before it is too late.
Children are able to develop and use their cognitive ability only if their arousal has been reduced by practicing self-regulation. We accomplish this by identifying and reducing stressors when they are hyperaroused and knowing what self-regulation strategies to use before it is too late.	Children get stimulated and aroused (this occurs in the limbic area or midbrain), which shuts down their thinking. When the limbic system is aroused, one of three things occurs: fight, flight, or fear.
Self-regulation speaks to the importance of reframing behavior, distinguishing between misbehavior and stress behavior. For that to be possible, we should recognize the signs of stress behavior.	Parenting advice centers on teaching children about the consequences of their actions and makes these lessons stick or how to build up a child's self-control.
The vital importance of self-regulation also tells us that we often talk (or worse) when we should be listening—with our eyes as much as our ears.	What neuroscience suggests is that kids learn less from lectures as opposed to doing tasks or applying what they learned.
Self-regulation reduces arousal and reaction to stimuli to bring back those reflective capacities.	Self-control reduces self-regulation, as it trumps self-regulation.

BEHAVIOR MODIFICATION

Good classroom management is synonymous with an effective behavior plan. Classroom management is extremely important. It sets the tone in the classroom as to what is acceptable and what is not or inappropriate behavior. The process begins with the teacher and students developing their classroom rules. This can be done with the class, as a school, or districtwide. Many school administrators prefer to have uniform procedures for classrooms that have commonalities such as "specials like art, music, physical education or grade-level rules." In this way students know what to expect in all of their classrooms.

The purpose of implementing uniform classroom management strategies is to enhance positive behavior and increase student academic engagement. Effective classroom management principles work across almost all subject areas and grade levels.

The Entire School Process

Schools that have implemented a schoolwide intervention policy have reported tremendous changes. When this happens and all stakeholders are committed to the program, the results are increased time for lessons, less bullying/conflicts, and more positive parent participation. It is the best way to approach establishing behavior expectations. With everyone, from custodians and cafeteria personnel to teachers and administrators, the quintessential task of setting up a good classroom management program lies in the consistency and continuity of the participants.

Classroom Rules

For responsibility, respect, expectations, and goals to be accomplished, it is imperative that you develop the rules of the classroom *with* the students. During the first week of class, begin to formulate the goals of the classroom. Tell the children that you have been observing "our classroom," and you have seen some great things and some *not* so great things going on and that it's time to make some rules in the classroom to keep everyone safe.

Ask them, "What are rules?" The answer should be similar to this: A rule helps us remember what is right and what is wrong. Rules keep things in order. Rules give us something called boundaries to help us keep our bodies to ourselves and keep our behavior positive. Sometimes, rules get broken, and when they do we learn so many things about ourselves and others.

As a class, begin scribing the rules on chart paper or your smart board. Children are very good at formulating rules. Be cognizant that the rules are very clear and concise without room for interpretation, which could represent inconsistencies or be misconstrued. Some rules are written, and others are unwritten, but the children usually know them all very well.

Below is an example of what your students may say:

- No hitting
- No kicking
- No tattling
- Report to help others
- Only one person speaks at a time
- No interrupting the teacher when he or she is talking
- No screaming or yelling inside and so on and so forth

Post Your Rules

Rules provide a sense of fairness to the students, but it is equally important to stress that fair is not equal. The rules represent expected behaviors, management for breaking the rules, expected social interactions, norms, and the school's climate and culture expectation for management of behavior. There is a difference between fair and equal. As the children become more mature and their comprehension improves, you will begin to hear words such as *respect*, *kind*, and *nice*. These words are known by many older children, but since we are building a whole group (or even school) rule chart, we will want to remain specific. Words such as *nice* and *kind* can be interpreted differently by each student.

Being nice to one person means something very different to another person. For instance, sharing a snack with me is being nice, but not hitting me is nice too! If you post the words *respect others* around the room, it is a good way to increase comprehension. In your rule chart, use the word *no* as often as possible. You will want to review these rules very often, and sometimes they will need to be reviewed daily.

Consequences

The Student Empowerment Program does not advocate punishments. The classroom, the teacher, and the students are in a new atmosphere that is calm, collected, fair, and trusting. The respect and character education traits have been developed, and the teacher is using her execution of the step-by-step process to ensure that the child is learning regulation. The children who are having "issues" will not be getting the attention from you or the others in the classroom. They will learn very quickly that the good behavior bee gets the honey. Behavioral consequences may be warranted. For instance, if a child calls another a name, then that name-caller will do something nice for the child whose feelings he hurt.

It's a Wrap

Once the rules have been established, begin to teach the breathing techniques. While you are teaching breathing, you are also teaching reflective strategies and mindfulness. The students will learn to regulate. Simultaneously, as the students are learning to regulate and display self-control, the teacher and support staff will be providing constructive feedback. This feedback will be understood by the children as clear and positive, and they will begin to learn that their positive actions get the positive attention of their teachers and peers. Responsibility and respect will develop, and self-regulation leads to classroom management.

Constantly observe the children and provide positive feedback. If the behavior needs help surfacing, you will need to "fake it a bit" *before* a negative behavior occurs. Don't catch the student being good; build a success before an issue happens. For instance, "You listened the first time I asked/I see that you are working cooperatively with your friend while you are playing together/You really look like you are serious about making the science experiment work/You sat next to your friend when you thought he looked sad/You are in great control of your hands today/Your mouth is biting food the way it should."

Make an effort to notice a student's behavior or effort. For example, "I noticed when you regrouped correctly in the hundreds column, you got the problem right." This comment reinforces expectations and correct skill practice. "I noticed you used the rubric on both of your assignments. You received an A, so your hard work paid off." Acknowledging students and the efforts they are making goes a long way to positively influence academic performance. Most people, and more specifically children, respond favorably to positive comments, and the positive comments reinforce behavioral expectations.

Adding Rules

You may also add new rules when something arises in the classroom that warrants it. Call a group meeting and say "I have witnessed something new happening in our classroom. Has anyone else seen the problem?" Then introduce and discuss your new rule. Behavioral consequences should not be given if a child does not know the rule, but you can add a new rule that was broken unknowingly. If a rule is broken and you really believe the child had no idea that he or she did something wrong, talk about it. Rules will transition into self-regulation, and you will find that rule discussions will diminish.

What Is Positive Feedback?

Feedback is any response from a teacher in regard to a student's performance or behavior. It can be verbal, written, or gestural. The purpose of positive feedback in the learning process is to improve a student's performance. The value of positive feedback, when it is given immediately, is that the student knows exactly what he or she did to get the feedback. The ultimate goal of positive feedback is to provide students with information that helps them continue positive behavior and extinguish negative behavior.

The use of negative body language, sarcasm, eye rolling, and huffing and puffing over student behavior is *not at all acceptable*. Students will always remember how you made them feel, and you do not want to demean or use put-downs. When you give feedback you are sending a positive message, and the child is learning to regulate behaviors due to your words.

The Dreaded Time-Out Chair

Time-out chairs are negative. It is not advisable to use them, as they have a poor connotation. Most three-, four-, and five-year-olds would not understand the concept of their use. They think they are bad. They do not realize it's the behavior that was not appropriate. They will think it is they who are bad. Renaming the chair "the thinking chair" would still have the same negative connotation. It is the negative attention and separation that you give that is inappropriate when you enforce a "chair" consequence.

Behavior Charts

Negative-type behavior charts and their variants are standard in elementary schools throughout the world. When we say negative, we mean the ones that "take away" what was already earned by the child. These charts have a punitive measure, such as going down a rung on a ladder, moving a space backward on the line, or erasing a checkmark that was already given. There are apps and technical programs for phones, as well as computers, that help the teacher track "good and bad behaviors," and they also keep track of points given and points taken away from the student. By using *The Student Empowerment Program* to its fullest potential, you will not have to resort to these negative methods.

It is not advisable to walk a child in the hallway or send a child to the principal for poor behavior. In actuality, when you send a child out of the room, you are sending a message to all the children that you cannot control the situation.

Of course, you must follow the protocol for a child who bites another child in class since this is a health issue.

Red Light, Green Light, No Light

Pass through the halls of almost any elementary school, and you are likely at some point to hear "pull a red ticket or you're on yellow. Keep up the good work; you are on green light now." These few words have such an impact on children. Negative behavior charts create stress, induce continued negative behavior, create anxiety in children, and cause outbursts from emotional standpoints, so *just don't use any light at all!*

Positive Forward-Moving Charts

The use of positive forward-moving behavior charts in the classroom do work. They encourage a quick change and can be used in conjunction with *The Student Empowerment Program*. The climate in your room is not competitive, so these charts will not be viewed that way. Actually, you will observe children cheering each other on as they move forward toward a common goal.

Some teachers do not believe that rewards, such as positive behavior charts or treasure boxes, should be used. *The Student Empowerment Program* does not need this support, but, if you feel that children learn from the external to internal motivations, then you will believe in rewards (not punishments). Some examples would be to move bees into the hive, spaceships toward the moon, and race cars around the track.

If you decide to use material awards from a treasure box, you can fade them out a bit at a time as your students move from extrinsic to intrinsic behavior modification responses. You may fade out the material rewards with extra computer time, playtime, reading time, or helping time; lunch with the teacher; or lunch with a friend in your room. The children will display an internalized feeling of regulation and no longer need the external rewards.

When you build your classroom from the ground up, you will begin to see changes in the environment and within the students, as well as the adults. There is a contagious flow of energy that each and every person will begin to feel. Your relationships with each other will become stronger and respect will abound.

The consequences are almost hidden among the positive outlook everyone displays. If a child is acting up or melting down, the other children in the classroom pay little mind to the child with the problem. At a later date, you will find peers helping each other deal with issues that bother them. They take their cue from the teacher role model, who remains cool, calm, and collected. If we paid no attention at the onset, by the time you began telling that troubled child that she is now breathing and controlling her body, she is already realizing that she is not being noticed by her peers. When the teacher begins stating that she is controlling herself, the child now realizes she is getting attention and will respond appropriately, as positive attention is better than no attention at all.

Setting Standards

Some of the changes you will begin to see once you have implemented *The Student Empowerment Program* can happen in just months after you begin. You may see changes in days, but those changes still need to be cemented in stone. It has been cited by professionals in both public and private schools that a new set of standards now exist after implementing the program.

More communication is apparent, and less angry moments happen. More positive than negative words are used, and the classroom is happy, safe, and thriving. The learning time increases as the disruptive behavior decreases. Test scores rise, and visits to the principal's office diminish. Parents request workshops to learn what to do at home.

Rubrics

The self-regulation of the children allows the teacher to begin to use rubrics, so that he or she may begin to transfer the responsibility of learning onto the child. Lines at the teacher's desk are nonexistent because the students have the regulatory skills to check their own learning level. Students attend to the rubric to find out how they can increase their quality of work toward excellence. Rubrics make all grading fair and encourage students to manage a new challenge of self without feeling pressured. They are in charge of their own learning. This is truly the nature of the learner in full force.

SUMMARY

To conclude, *The Student Empowerment Program* is a whole-child program. It is the result of many years of experience in the classroom, many experiences in summer camp programs, and many college classes on childhood development at Kean University. It was years spent as a father and coach to four sons, assistant superintendent of curriculum, superintendent of schools, and a professor at Kean University. Together, Dr. Barbiere and Jane Wiatr, realized that their combination of experience created a brain research–based student empowerment program, which has been helping many teachers, staff members, administrators, and parents over the years.

The Student Empowerment Program sets the stage for positive classroom management. This chapter has been described in detail, so that you can begin to implement it as soon as possible. There is no need to wait to use it. Start at the beginning, and make changes a little at a time. Let positive thoughts spill over into your responses through language with whoever you meet. Upon entering your first day of school, remember to breathe, take it step by step, shoot for the moon, and, if you fall off the star, get back on. You do not have to wait to start tomorrow like a bad diet plan; start from the moment you slip, and move forward with your head up. You can always start your day over at any time. Change it immediately to a more positive outlook. "I think I can" said the Little Blue Engine, and he did.

Chapter Two

The Nature of the Learner and the Early Childhood Learning Brain

FOCUS OF THE CHAPTER

This chapter will describe the nature of the learner, so that teachers, support staff, and administrators understand how a student learns in a developmentally appropriate manner and how to teach to different learning styles. We will combine early childhood education strategies and *The Student Empowerment Program* with the nature of the learner so that a strong base of knowledge is formed for all stakeholders. Finally, we will focus on the learning brain model and how it applies to learning and teaching while keeping the nature of the learner in mind.

FOCUS QUESTIONS FOR THE CHAPTER

1. What is meant by "the nature of the learner"?
2. How does the nature of the learner use developmentally appropriate practice and learning styles in its instructional pedagogy?
3. How does the nature of the learner support *The Student Empowerment Program*?
4. How does brain research play an integral role in the development of the nature of the learner?
5. Is the learning brain model related to the nature of the learner?

DEFINE THE NATURE OF THE LEARNER

When we think about the nature of the learner, we think about the cognitive, social, and emotional characteristics of the student and how information is processed by the student. There has been much brain research conducted providing insights into how students learn and enabling teachers to develop lessons based on how the learner learns. Applying this knowledge allows the teacher to employ strategies that engender a more effective lesson.

Students will want to learn when the material presented has sense and meaning to them. But, when students are not presented with material that has meaning, they disengage from the learning activity. For instance, teachers understand that certain questions show disinterest, such as when a student states "Why are we learning this? Will this be on the test? When will I use this?" These questions send up a red flag for teachers, which tells them the students do not see value in the intended learning or it doesn't make sense to them. Knowing how the learner processes information will enable the teacher to design lessons that promote learning. It begins with establishing the learning environment.

Your child learns best by *actively engaging with the environment*. This includes:

- Providing a rich and stimulating environment to encourage curiosity, problem solving, and activity.
- Promoting student observation of surroundings.
- Encouraging listening skills.
- Asking "stretching" questions to promote metacognition (i.e., why).
- Asking open-ended questions to promote metacognition.
- Experimenting with textures, objects, and materials, such as water or sand.
- Stimulating the senses through touch, taste, smell, vision, and hearing.

Students also learn by being *involved in their own learning*. This could be as simple as:

- Choosing books to read.
- Pointing to pictures in books.
- Choosing objects and toys with which to play.
- Self-regulating their learning.
- Making choices regarding likes and dislikes.

For children to learn effectively and be successful, the teacher must have multiple data points regarding the students' personalities, multiple intelligences, and strengths and weaknesses. Evaluating all of this information will enable the teacher to differentiate her lesson based on the student's skill level and needs. The reflection of the student by the teacher, as well as the feedback toward the student's success, is what defines the nature of the learner.

Critical points for teachers to remember include self-regulation skills for the student by modeling self-regulation strategies, using oral rehearsal, or sharing the strategies with the students as you do a task, so they can see what the process looks like using prompts and cues and withdrawing your support at the appropriate time, so they become more empowered.

And now your classroom, or is it the Peanuts gang? The genius artistry and creativity of Charles Schultz brought the infamous Peanuts gang to life in the 1950s. If you had the opportunity to read Schultz's comics or view the TV shows, then you most likely remember the characters Charlie Brown, Lucy, Peppermint Patty, Linus, Schroeder, Pig Pen, and others.

As you enter your classroom, you probably won't be surprised to find that you are faced with an exuberant classroom of Charlie Browns, Lucys, and Linuses in the real world.

Did Mr. Schultz know that he created a typical classroom of students when he ingeniously invented the characters of his comic strip series? According to all accounts, Charles Schulz fashioned his characters after people who were close to his heart and people with whom he worked and went to school.

PEANUTS GANG AND THE NATURE OF THE LEARNER

Each character in the Peanuts gang is symbolic of a personality of your students, students whom you will get to know, teach, support, and guide. Accordingly, you need to understand how they learn, so you can effectively address their needs.

As we discuss the nature of the learner, be cognizant of the students in your own classroom, and begin the reflection process of getting to know the nature of your students. For the purpose of this chapter, if you are not familiar with Charlie Brown and the Peanuts Gang, use this link to read about the humorous group of children: https://www.psychologytoday.com/us/blog/and-all-jazz/201003/the-charlie-brown-theory-personality.

Critical cognitive factors regarding the nature of the learner:

- Some students are auditory and understand language better this way than when they speak.
- Students are interested in the present. Vague concepts of past/future lack meaning to them. Planning requires lessons that make sense and have meaning.
- Provide activities that promote engagement, so students become eager to learn.
- Scaffolding questions promotes discussion and should bring students to a higher level of metacognition.
- Students learn by doing.
- Teachers should develop a sense of humor, no sarcasm.

- Students communicate best when arranged in a small group of peers. They may require guidance from an adult when starting a new task.

Examples of innate dispositions that children possess and need to be developed:

- Creativity: Teachers should encourage students to be expressive and have freedom to inspire self.
- Social skills: Teachers should encourage collaboration and communication with peers.
- Resilience: Students build stamina and become independent through trial and error.
- Resourcefulness: Students will seek out opportunities and exploration to promote self-regulation and independence.
- Confidence: As students work on projects and are successful, they develop their sense of self.

HOW TO LEARN ABOUT YOUR STUDENTS

Teachers need to know what makes the child learn successfully in and out of school. The key to the child's success is to focus our teaching style on the nature of the learner. Yes, out of school is important as well, and we call this type of learning "home learning." Children have affects that they bring to school, some good and some not so good, that impact learning.

Teachers should be aware of how the brain collects, stores, uses, and scaffolds information, so that they may become specialized at the individual's needs and find an effective way to teach the student. Without this data, it is very difficult to correctly teach the young child. For instance, one important concept to keep in mind is that the brain consolidates information when the person sleeps. This makes the utmost difference in material delivery since information sent home with the child must be correct and if so, it will lead to consolidation.

GETTING TO KNOW YOU

The teacher's first step is to learn about the student in general. You may decide to do a personality survey or an "I am . . . " fill-in-the-blank worksheet with an older student, and with the younger student you may "share" at circle time allowing the students to discuss their feelings. Both of these suggestions provide the teacher with needed information and help to determine whether the child is ready for learning.

Your observation and data collection determine how the child interacts with others in large and small groups or if the child plays alone. Does the child sit in the closet or hide under his desk? Is the child covering his ears at loud noises? You will be collecting notes throughout the day to gain a better understanding of strengths and weaknesses of your learner.

You may have a large class of students, but it is imperative that you do this for all students to gain more information about how they learn. Monitor behaviors, problem-solving skills, interactions with adults, how they answer questions, and so forth and so on. Observable information from safe, secure environments is 10-fold in its value because it is the child in a positive, natural learning situation and children need a safe environment to learn.

Students are a varied mix of personalities and developmental, cognitive, social, and emotional levels. Just look at the personalities in the Peanuts gang. Those characters are a representation of your classroom. You may enter to find that your classroom is a mix of children who are gifted and talented, below grade level, disorganized, undiagnosed and diagnosed ADD, extroverts, introverts, ELL learners, noncommunicative children, special needs children/spectrum, children with "baggage," so-called head of household children, or even depressed personalities. All of these characteristics affect how the child learns. The key to the student's success is the ability of the teacher to build appropriate lessons, based on how individual children learn, and to understand what goals and objectives must be conquered through differentiated instruction.

A teacher may be assigned a third-grade class and know that, typically, third-graders will learn multiplication, will reference in research papers, and love Harry Potter books, but this is a huge generalization. This background profile is imperative, as it provides a better understanding of individual expectations. As you already know, it is different for every learner, and it is the teacher's responsibility to unlock the door to the child's learning potential through data collection and lesson design.

HOWARD GARDNER AND MULTIPLE INTELLIGENCES

Once you develop a background profile of each of your students, you may find using the theory of multiple intelligences is warranted to address the student's various "intelligences." Multiple intelligences is the theory of Howard Gardner, who identified how each of us learns. His research found that everyone learns differently and that our use of "minds" is the reason why people perform and understand in various ways. His theory includes eight multiple intelligence categories: visual-spatial, body-kinesthetic, musical, logical-mathematical, interpersonal, intrapersonal, naturalist, and linguistic. It would be advisable to do a multiple intelligence survey of your students in order to find out how your scholar learns. It is also most likely that they will score in more than one of the categories noted.

ASSESSMENTS

Some schools allow observation to stand alone as an assessment strategy, especially in private prekindergarten, but if you are in a public school or a private school with a curriculum for math and reading then most likely you will be evaluating the child with a standardized test. It's important to give this test early in the school year, but not before you have allowed the student to acclimate himself to the safe environment. You may begin once you observe the child thriving.

Remember, not all children thrive the same way. A child with special needs may never thrive as comfortably as a regular-developing peer, so use your judgment as to when the child has become comfortable enough to be tested. Always instruct the child beforehand on how to "fill in the bubbles," and do not put undue pressure on the child. Be a calm role model, and communicate that the "test" or "paperwork" is for you. It's only for you, so that you can help the child learn better. This is a very true statement and may help relieve any stress the child feels about testing situations.

When gathering data about academic levels it is important to know when the child is ready to learn. Some of your participants may be prereaders and will score as such on the assessments, and others may have come to school as strong readers and score two or three grade levels above age level in reading and comprehension. Both of these are good examples of understanding the nature of the learner. At this time, you will also discover speech issues, ELL needs, or even whether a child needs glasses. A lot is learned during one-on-one assessments.

Once you have gained this valuable information, it will be your opportunity to begin building connections and start using your learner's strengths to increase knowledge. You now have a learning profile of your student, and you will be able to work with the nature of the learner in social, emotional, and cognitive domains of learning, by using your best practice skills in a developmentally appropriate way.

You may be thinking to yourself, how will I address multiple intelligences, background profile information, and results of assessments and still do it well?

THE BALANCING ACT

In a large classroom setting it becomes a balancing act of children's educational levels, as well as developmental levels, mixed with their wants and needs. You will be tapping into what makes your learner tick. You will be looking at challenges for your learner, as well as what is challenging.

After all of your observation, reflection, data collection, and assessments, you will begin the process of sorting it out, calculating medians and learning curves, and finally using good old common sense. Your common sense has a foundation in all the preliminary work you did to understand the milestones and sequence of development of a child. Now, planning and identifying activities, providing appropriate environmental experiences, using multiple intelligences to the best of your ability, and implementing strategies and techniques will promote growth and learning.

Your lesson design will be your guide from general to specific objectives. *The Student Empowerment Program* will help you with classroom management and student regulation. Be sure not to cease *The Student Empowerment Program* just because you think all is perfect. It is an ongoing process and should never stop, as the positive is welcomed all the time. Once all is in place, it will not be hard to focus on individual needs in a differentiated way. You may find grouping children in heterogeneously or homogeneously groups works better, depending upon what you are teaching.

SCENARIOS

These five scenarios will test your knowledge about the nature of the learner. Read each question first and then the scenarios.

1. What is each of the underlying characteristics of the learner?
2. Do you know what to do if these students were in your classroom?
3. What attainable goals will you set for these students?
4. What plan of action will you take?

THE FIVE SCENARIOS

Kindergarten: Teacher: He cannot build a vertical tower with blocks and could not read the easiest of the sight word cards.

1st Grade: Teacher: He is behind in reading, he was not focused, and he could not sit still and is always out of his seat.

2nd Grade: Teacher: She calls out and does not follow along when we use the smart board. She loses her place when she reads and cannot copy from the board.

3rd Grade: Teacher: He is a distraction. He throws his pencil on the ground and talks to the child in the seat next to him all day long. He gets up whenever he wants and talks out of turn. I have moved him many times to other areas of the room; now I want to move him out of the room!

4th Grade: Teacher: He can't do division. He can't do fractions either. His test scores are below 30%. He is failing math.

Please give your answers serious consideration as if these were students in your classroom.

Table 2.2 is the chart to fill in your answers. Table 2.1 is our solutions. Our solutions are not written in stone, and your answers may be the same or even better than what we planned for the students. You are invited to think about the nature of the learner, the foundation of child development, developmentally appropriate practices, *The Student Empowerment Program*, and all of the information provided for you in this book in order to construct your best answers.

Table 2.1. Action Plan for Five Scenarios

Grade	Problem	Missing Piece	Solution
Kindergarten	Cannot build a tower of 10 vertical blocks.	Balance ability/maturation of body development slightly weak. Weak core development. Hand–eye coordination weak and hand movements immature.	One-on-one help. Build against the wall for support. Build with a partner. Keep working at it and have fun when blocks fall down. Build gradually and slowly. Note that the child built two blocks, then three, then four, etc. each day.
	Cannot understand simple words.	No sense and meaning. Black and white writing on cards. No consistent formation of letter by teacher. Use of "*a*" instead of the primary "**a**."	Create sense and meaning by using kinesthetic intelligence. Make body parts letters by bending into an A and M shape for the word *am*. Use word cards with opposite color spectrum words and cards (e.g., purple word and yellow background).
	Behind in reading.	Forgot kindergarten sight words—retest.	Reteach kindergarten sight words.
	Not focused.	School nurse's eye-screening records. Suggested retest of eye exam if no improvement by nurse. Retest leveled reader level.	Parents consented to taking child to a private ophthalmologist for extensive eye exam. Leveled reader—use one level below "too hard." Build success in reading. Use index card to read line by line. Child received eyeglasses in a month.
1st Grade	Cannot sit still and always out of his seat.	Young student, early birthday. Needs movement and redirection to focus. More attention given to correct behaviors needed. Desk work as opposed to group table work. Lack of multiple ways of teaching reading (i.e., group, partner, read aloud, oral reading, taped reading, smart board books). Movement needed in classroom. No brain breaks.	Provide child with cushion wiggle seat and allow child to move when necessary. Hands-on activities for subject matter. Smart board and other media as alternatives for learning. Make child "in charge, leader" in class. Teach rules the Student Empowerment Program (SEP) way.

(continued)

Table 2.1. (continued)

Grade	Problem	Missing Piece	Solution
2nd Grade	Calls out, not in turn. Does not follow along on pages. She loses her place when she reads and cannot copy from the board.	No purposeful scheduled time to chat. No downtime. Constant work all morning until lunch.	Teacher consented to use of brain breaks, scheduled chatting time, Pandora radio transition times, and less teacher-directed activities. More child-directed and teacher-facilitated activities.
	Student desk is sideways and does not face the board so it is hard to turn body and write.	Student desk stayed in same area, but turned so it was facing board.
		Credit system set up in class to teach positive rules. Employ Student Empowerment Program.
3rd Grade	Distracted and a distraction. Throws pencil. Out of seat constantly. Does not follow rules of the classroom. Bothers others.	Hyper-type child. Behavioral issues. Emotional luggage when entered school. Cultural and social issues interfere with learning. No safe or secure feeling in classroom based on early experiences in school. Drug-related birth.	SEP initiated in classroom with all staff members involved with student all day long. Plan for child to visit principal for positive emotional stress relief. Credit system. Parent part of action plan. Positive rule setting and recognition. Regulation and mindfulness training.
4th Grade	Cannot do division or fractions.	Retest addition, subtraction, and multiplication facts.	Resulted in not being able to add without manipulatives. Retaught addition facts and multiplication facts on smart board math games. Subtraction was hindered by the inability to add, although this was not observed by the teacher, but observed by action committee. Fractions were taught by using games.
	Low test scores, 30% or below.	Too many problems on a page. Student overwhelmed with failure and inability to find a place to start. Immediate shutdown to test.	Quizzes given instead of tests in smaller increments.
	Failing math.	Child turned off and scared of math since so many failures.	Quizzes included addition and multiplication division. Test scores improved self-esteem up

Table 2.2.

Grade	Problem	Missing Piece	Solution

SUMMARY

In this chapter, the nature of the learner was defined. The formula for learning about the nature of the learner was discussed. As noted, the teacher focuses her understanding of how her learner learns and how to teach her learner once she has collected her data. Howard Gardner's multiple intelligences, student profiles, and student assessment were combined to give the teacher a strong foundation of information in order to know the nature of the learner.

Application of the information was delivered in a scenario format, so that the reader could attempt to formulate answers and maximize learning for the scholar. Teaching and learning were addressed by incorporating *The Student Empowerment Program*, developmentally appropriate practice, and differentiated instruction.

Chapter Three

The Classroom Environment and the Early Childhood Learning Brain

FOCUS OF THE CHAPTER

The chapter begins unpacking the learning environment and *The Student Empowerment Program* and its relationship to the classroom environment. Establishing the classroom environment is the first step to ensure program effectiveness and begin establishing the learning domain. The role of climate, environment, emotional security, mood, and classroom management need to addressed and in place for an effective *Student Empowerment Program* and strong, positive, and controlled classroom management.

FOCUS QUESTIONS FOR THE CHAPTER

1. How do I want my scholars to behave in my classroom and in common areas?
2. What role do I play in regulating student behavior?
3. What are the strategies students can use to self-regulate their behavior?
4. How do I establish my learning environment to promote student participation?
5. How does the Learner's Brain Model (figure 3.1) correlate to *The Student Empowerment Program* (figure 3.2)?
6. What is the impact of student self-regulation to behavior and academics within the classroom setting?

INTRODUCTION

This chapter will define the components of *The Student Empowerment Program* as it relates to the classroom environment. The classroom climate and atmosphere must be established to set expectations and regulate student behavior and learning. Empowering students in this approach enables them to make intelligent decisions, use their words to address problems, and modulate

36 • CHAPTER THREE

their behavior to ensure comprehensive skill building, as well as become adept at the formal learning process.

It is our intention to provide you with all of the information you will need to set up a positive classroom through the use of *The Student Empowerment Program*, with clear objectives that are productive and promote learning. The goal is for you to feel comfortable in your teaching, while building professional relationships with your students. When you employ this method in your classroom environment, you will be well on your way to becoming a master at your trade.

Figure 3.1. Pyramid Learner's Brain Model

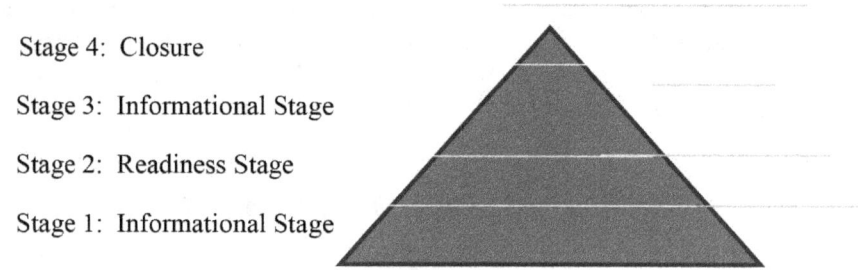

The Learner's Brain Model

Stage 4: Closure

Stage 3: Informational Stage

Stage 2: Readiness Stage

Stage 1: Informational Stage

Figure 3.2. Flow Chart Student Empowerment Program
The Student Empowerment Program

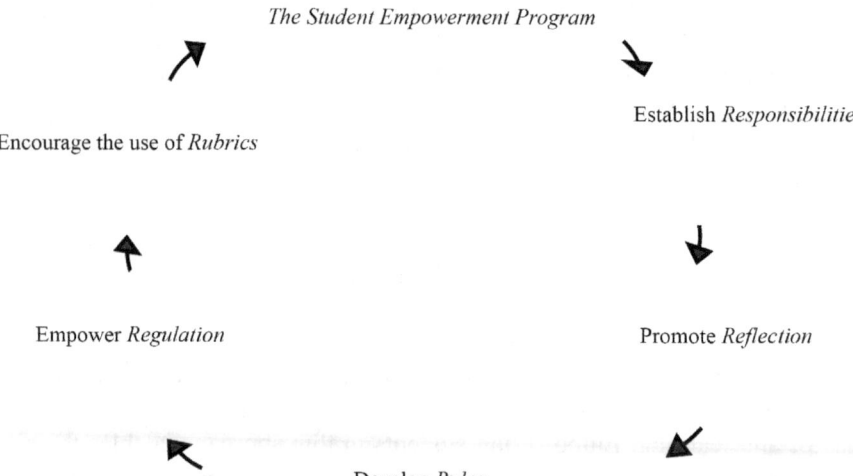

The Student Empowerment Program

Encourage the use of *Rubrics*

Establish *Responsibilities*

Empower *Regulation*

Promote *Reflection*

Develop *Rules*

DEVELOP RULES

Prior to incorporating *The Student Empowerment Program* into your classroom, you will want to think about your classroom and your whole-child approach to teaching. It is imperative that you begin to consider how to build a classroom of students that is positive; supports emotional, cognitive, and social learning; and is effective and self-regulated. As important, the physical space must be child and adult friendly, conducive to learning, and safe and secure.

IN THE BEGINNING: YOU AND YOUR PHILOSOPHY OF EDUCATION

As an educator, your philosophy of education will most likely reflect one of our great educational theorists, such as John Dewey, Maria Montessori, or Reggio Emilia. These theorists had a great amount of information written about them, and parts of their theories discussed the teaching and learning environment.

Dewey believed that the environment for teaching and learning should be "simplified, purified, balanced and steadying." Emilia Reggio believed that the environment is a tool for the teacher, as well as an additional teacher in the classroom. The relationship the child has with her environment is crucial in the Emilia Reggio approach to teaching. Maria Montessori believed that hands-on learning equaled success and that the classroom design and furniture, as well as the manipulatives used by the student, should reflect high quality, just like a carpenter's tools, so the child becomes familiar with real-life examples.

These are just three theorists who, as an early childhood teacher, you may be familiar with and hold in high regard. Upon further investigation, you can conclude that all three of these theorists overlap in their theories, and you may use their theories when developing a positive climate in your classroom.

OPEN-SPACE SCHOOL CONCEPT

The open-space school concept was first introduced into the United States in 1965 as an experimental, elementary school classroom configuration whereby the physical walls separating classrooms were removed to promote movement across class areas by teachers. Advocates of open-plan schools argued that students should be allowed to learn in ways suited to their individual differences and that the most effective teaching and learning strategies allowed teachers to work collaboratively with each other and team-teach, hence, the removal of classroom walls. Teachers were encouraged to work with colleagues and track students from year to year. Open classrooms focused on students "learning by doing" resonated with those who believed that America's formal, teacher-led classrooms were inhibiting students' creativity.

CAMPUS SCHOOL/EXPERIMENTAL SCHOOL/ OPEN-SPACE CLASSROOM

A northern New Jersey college decided to implement an open-classroom model on the college campus. The Campus School's philosophy of education and teaching pedagogy was quite different from the traditional classroom one thought of during the mid-1960s. During that time, if you attended a traditional classroom, desks were in rows, and the atmosphere of the classroom left much to be desired. Campus School was nontraditional, open, and innovative.

This school was inclusive, or integrated with general and special education students. The school accepted special needs children long before inclusion in the state of New Jersey was law, with the inclusion model of education, like we know it today.

The classroom was designed with no walls, similar to many Head Start classrooms. It had two large "bathtubs" in the middle of the room that housed turtles, fish, frogs, and toads. All the teachers, as well as the principal of the school, were professors from the college. Children played and worked outside in a contained courtyard, as well as inside.

Children learned by conversation, higher-level thinking strategies, and connecting prior knowledge to new knowledge to expand their learning (scaffolding). The major difference between how the students of the Campus School learned and how the public school students learned was the amount of play and exploration, creativity, and personal reflection, which were part of the program throughout the years.

THE HEAD START ENVIRONMENT

Head Start began in 1965. The program was part of Lyndon B. Johnson's Great Society campaign. The campaign provided a large amount of funding for early childhood programs, deemed to be comprehensive to meet the needs of disadvantaged children, who would not otherwise be exposed to a developmentally appropriate preschool program at three and four years of age. The

Head Start classroom was designed to "flow," with smooth transitions, and used learning centers toward self-regulatory skills.

The Head Start classroom was focused on building a community with "no walls" and was structured in such a way that it provided social interaction for the development of cognition. The majority of the day was child centered/child directed and teacher facilitated.

ATMOSPHERE AND LEARNING

The essential question "What creates an atmosphere that is conducive to learning?" contains the key components to all of the other questions and their answers.

The question's answer is seemingly quite obvious, as it is the beginning, the end, and everything in between. There is no simple, clearly defined answer, but many integrated components that are part of the establishment of a positive atmosphere.

Your classroom atmosphere should be inviting and enriching. It should be a classroom where lesson engagement is a critical part of the day, and it should encompass many reflective activities, ascertain clear communication skills, and subject the students to inference and critical thinking, as well as hypothesizing.

It is an environment that is warm, accepting, educationally sound and socially acceptable, and most importantly, one that is conducive to learning.

ESTABLISH A SAFE ENVIRONMENT

It is imperative to create a safe learning environment for the students. The positive relationships that you build with staff and between staff and students are regarded as essential to establishing an environment that is conducive to learning. Building a community within your classroom alerts the students to the fact that you are a good listener, an organized planner, a positive role model, and more. Send them positive "vibes" while you sit and talk to them. Play background music as often as you can in order to set the mood of the day or activity. Music can signal when work time is starting or ending, as well as its having a collaborative, calming effect on the students. A controlled (not controlling), self-assured teacher who presents her students with a judgment-free atmosphere, as well as kindness, tolerance, patience, fairness, and humor (not sarcasm), has the potential to begin her school year on a positive note and continue that feeling throughout the school year.

The teacher must celebrate achievements in her students as well. Here is an example. Student M had such a wonderful story to tell, which exemplifies the nature of the learner in a safe and nurturing environment. This scenario is true, and you will see how children can affect the climate of the classroom. The teachers' responses in this case are of the utmost importance.

STUDENT M'S STORY

Here is the story of a very precocious child who shared that his mother was having a baby and that he was going to be a big brother. The children and teachers were quite happy with his share, and *he* was glowing with pride. His announcement ignited his brain to continue to critically think, and he was exploring his important thoughts.

He announced that the baby was going to be named Oops. The teachers replied, "Oh, Student M, that is wonderful; we can see how proud you are to be a big brother." The teachers understood that the child's enthusiasm for speaking in front of the group was monumental, and they were careful not to squelch this important moment. With no prompting, he continued to use his language and literacy skills to the best of his ability.

The teachers listened patiently and readied themselves to interject if the story took a turn that was less appropriate for preschoolers. Student M proceeded to tell that his brother, in the belly, was not "planned" and that he was an "oops" baby. His final statements from his sharing time were just as his dad had told him; that's the reason the baby will be named Oops!

In this case, there were no major surprises, and the teachers were comfortable with how they formed a safe classroom environment. The children were accepting and understood as much as they needed about babies. The teachers allowed Student M to report and accepted his share with a warm smile and a big hug of happiness (your school will have rules about hugging and touching). The other children followed suit by hugging him in a congratulatory manner. The teachers acknowledged his "achievement" as he certainly owned the moment. The teachers remained neutral (a neutral position sends a clear message that everything is OK to all of the students in the classroom), as any sign of distress or anguish could have turned this simple statement into more than it actually was intended by Student M.

This was *the* ultimate teachable moment, and Student M was given the emotional support and respect from both his peers and the adults in the room. Body language, positive verbal responses/feedback, exhibits of acceptance, and reflective listening ears allowed the rest of the children to feel like parts to the whole in Student M's world.

When a teacher is comfortable in her own skin, situations and experiences like these do *not* "rattle" her; instead, they open up doors to learning.

The following is our real-life example of how you can take a simple "sharing time" and build it into a full-length Project Approach lesson, which increases the positive climate of the classroom. It highlights the teacher's ability to connect with the students; it depicts "teachable moments" with no formal lesson planned (initially), and it shows how the positive atmosphere of the classroom aided in total engagement of the children.

NEXT STEP: EXTEND THE LEARNING TO CREATE AN ATMOSPHERE CONDUCIVE TO CONTINUAL LEARNING

During guided play Student M's mommy visited, so that the children could listen to the baby's heartbeat and feel the baby kick with their hands. Materials such as stethoscopes, bottles, blankets, cribs, burping clothes, high chairs, plastic baby food containers, and other everyday baby-related items were easily accessible to the children and were of high caliber (similar to Montessori products) so that they worked properly, were strong, and could sustain a lot of use.

The housekeeping center contained developmentally appropriate toys, books, and items to learn about babies, bellies, families, feedings, diapering, and more. The children bathed rubber baby dolls and diapered and feed them as part of the unstructured free play in our classroom. Extra mirrors were provided so the children could watch themselves at work.

At the housekeeping center, children were busy learning, as well as building their own competence, through self-directed play in that area. This play was unstructured, and teachers did not interfere, but allowed those who had brothers and sisters and had been through this process to teach their peers the age-appropriate lessons of life. Again, their language was developmental, and most of what was being acted out was reflective of what the children observed at home or were invited to do during helping times with baby brothers and sisters.

Health and wellness, nutrition, and many other objectives were written in daily and monthly lesson planning. This Project Approach lesson design was complete, and its value was immense for learning (see chapter 5 for more information). The classroom atmosphere was busy and directed by the children. Goal-setting strategies were introduced, and months of pregnancy were counted in math activities. There was time for investigation and inquiry, as well as skill development.

HOW IS THIS SCENARIO AN EXAMPLE OF THE POSITIVE CLASSROOM ENVIRONMENT?

The collaboration and cooperation were strong between students and their peers, and a positive "air" was seen by all who entered the classroom. Acceptance, tolerance, diversity, integrity, honesty, and all of their counterparts make up the part of the classroom that is not physical, like chairs and tables. An environment was established that was open and accepting from the first day of school; students were comfortable speaking about topics of interest. The classroom transformed in such a way that creativity and critical thinking were steadily and readily increasing.

Body and verbal language send a salient message to your students. Demeanor means so much to the children. They can "read" you like a book. You will begin to build relationships with the students that make them feel important and valuable to the classroom. Learning about the nature of the learner (see chapter 2 for more information) is equally important.

The collaboration between students taught social and emotional skills, and the cooperation between parent and students brought in a real-world experience for new cognitive development.

The feeling that was generated in the classroom was inclusive and "wholistic" in nature. Every child, staff member, and parent knew that, no matter what they did or said, they would be accepted and diversity abounded.

THE PHYSICAL ENVIRONMENT

The physical environment is a direct image of your planning for student learning. The classroom is where both teacher and student spend most of their time. It is a place students can call their own and reflect upon their expectations. It should be purposefully organized, comfortable, and student friendly, so that the environment is conducive for learning. The environment is established with a variety of manipulatives for cognitive, social, emotional, and physical development. The learning environment promotes student self-regulation. It and all the other components that have been discussed in this book help solidify the positive environment. The environment is both nature and nurture, and the teacher needs to remain cognizant of this.

THE IDEA OF A POSITIVE CLASSROOM CLIMATE INCLUDES ARRANGEMENT AND FLOOR PLAN

When arranging the room, you want to provide a safe room arrangement, one that does not distract students from learning, but enriches the way to meet the learning objective, as well as the desire of the student population to learn. The relationship of the teacher to students, in addition to the relationships of the students to each other, is also an important factor in your positive classroom.

POSITIVE CLASSROOM AND ROOM ARRANGEMENT

When developing guidelines for preschool teachers, the state of New Jersey (and other states) has guidelines for developing the physical environment of the classroom. The physical environment of a preschool classroom has an impact on both the behavior and learning of the children and adults working in that space. The environment must be consistent with the teaching pedagogy. When an administrator walks past the door of the teacher's classroom, she may formulate ideas of the classroom, just by noticing the good or poor structure of the arrangement. For example, if the administrator sees straight rows of desks, she may think that this teacher uses a lecture-only, direct instructional approach to teaching. When viewing a classroom where the teacher is on the floor, that administrator will perceive a hands-on environment.

States and townships may set minimum square footage for students, so that there are no more students than the maximum allowed by law. Although square footage is established, financial constraints and growing enrollments may sometimes cause overcrowded classrooms. The fire marshal of your town makes scheduled school visits, but will make additional visits to a school if he sees that classrooms are overcrowded and deemed unsafe for students.

Crowded classrooms may create a decline in learning, as they are usually disorganized, have poor classroom management, and face demanding challenges as student numbers increase. As long as your administration is not breaking the law with student enrollment, you can address a crowded classroom by keeping lessons short, making sure students are engaged, and actively participating in the activities, using flexible grouping, and setting up a positive atmosphere. In the case of large numbers of children in your classroom, you will continue to maintain focus and pace yourself, as well as continue to teach children to become self-regulated as early as possible.

The optimal classroom environment allows children to have independent access to materials and activities and plenty of space for movement. The classroom environment should have learning centers that encourage children's experiences with blocks, books, dramatic play, creative arts, writing, manipulatives, math, science, sand, water, and computers. Space should accommodate both active and quiet activities. Soft furnishings and spaces for quiet times should be available for children who need a place to rest or read.

Adequate physical space affects children's levels of involvement and the types of interactions with their teachers and peers. Classrooms for preschool children must be designed specifically to meet the needs of three- and four-year-old children and allow movement in the classroom.

When constructing a classroom, you will want to reflect upon the composition of the physical room environment. An open classroom floor plan, as well as a classroom with minimal boundaries, has been provided for you. The teacher can use the walls of the classroom to environmentally construct the learning environment to promote self-regulation.

The "ECERS–R, PCMI, SELA Rating Scale" is a valuable tool when assessing the structure and design of the room. This rating scale is a comprehensive assessment tool that can be used as you prepare you centers and classroom. It will assist you while you optimize the amount of learning in all areas of the curriculum. (The information source for the original document is https://www.nj.gov/education/ece/checkups/checklist.pdf, Early Childhood Environment Rating Scale Early Childhood Enrichment, as per the internet article).

Figure 3.3 is a drawing of a suggested floor plan, which lends itself to an open- or semi-open concept of learning. Please note that the line you see to the right side of the floor plan is imaginary for some, and, for others, it may be a "pony wall." The floor plan is not to scale, but it will allow you to understand the ebb and flow of the room, one that you will want in your physical space arrangement in order to maximize learning and create an atmosphere conducive to learning.

Here are some considerations as you set up your classroom environment:

1. Plan the traffic flow from one center to the next center, so there is no congestion or "bottlenecks" between the centers.
2. Centers should have specific objectives or goals in mind. They should be purposefully developed and constructed.
3. Provide directions at the centers (pictures, written, or oral/compact disc) so students will know what to do when they get to the center.
4. Have "challenge" activities available for students who finish early.

THE CLASSROOM ENVIRONMENT AND THE EARLY CHILDHOOD LEARNING BRAIN • 45

5. The classroom should be safe and free from obstacles to avoid injury to the children.
6. Follow state and local regulations and laws pertaining to fire safety, sanitization, and bathroom facilities, as well as lighting ventilation and temperature control.
7. If you prefer not to have an open classroom, use the furniture, such as rolling carts of blocks, to divide your room. Please make sure that children cannot fall over carts or rolling walls and that they cannot fall upon the children. Safety first.

Figure 3.3. Room Arrangement

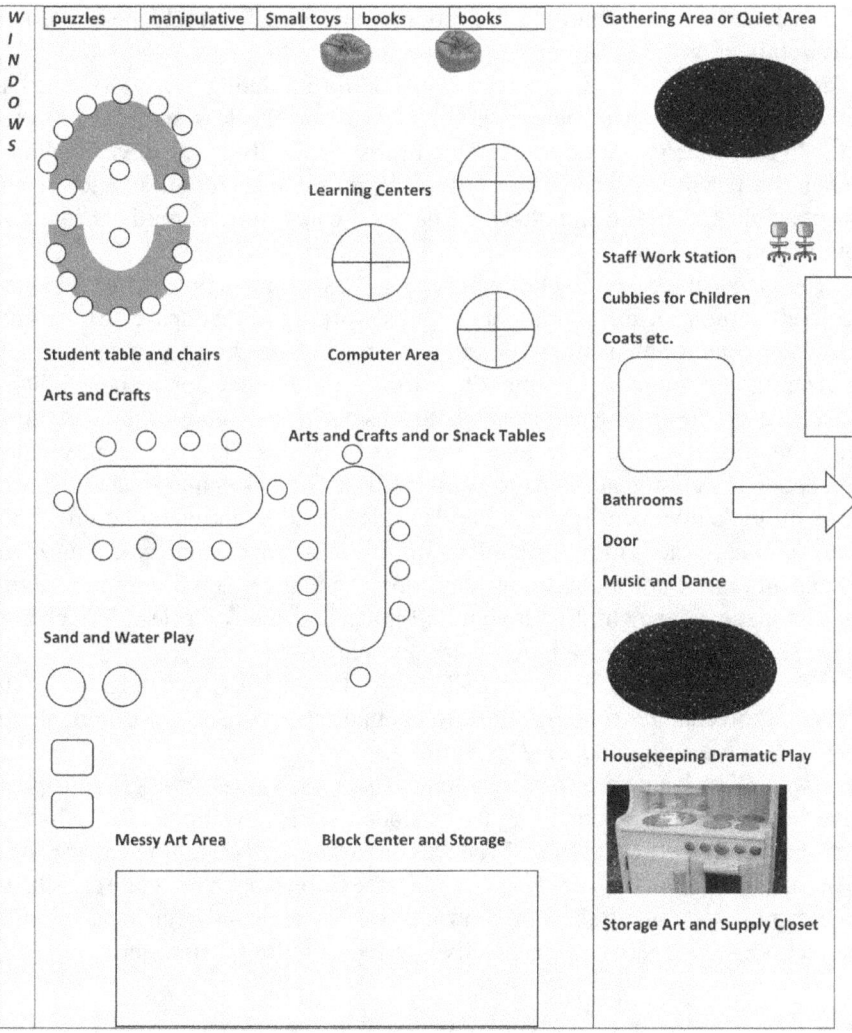

8. Consideration should be given to noisy activity centers, so as not to disturb quiet centers.

THE STUDENT EMPOWERMENT PROGRAM AND THE 5RS

How do the 5Rs (responsibility, reflection, rules, regulation, and rubrics) affect the classroom climate? They personally affect the student, but in reality they are also part of the teacher, support staff, parents, administrators, all stakeholders, and *the classroom environment. The Student Empowerment Program* (chapter 1) is a "wholistic" approach to education. Below you will find a few thoughts regarding the program and how it affects the classroom environment.

Responsibility: The teacher is responsible for modeling behaviors. She has a responsibility to plan, implement, and evaluate the lessons that she presents to the students. Another example of responsibility to the environment is when the teacher is setting up or cleaning up the classroom. The teacher is responsible for and to the students, parents, caregivers, administration, and other staff members.

The physical environment of a classroom has an impact on both the behavior and learning of the children and adults working in that space. An optimal classroom environment allows children to have independent access to materials and activities, and more importantly, it can be used to develop responsibility.

Reflection is established through the use of mindfulness and breathing, and this positive reflection determines the "air" of calm and serenity when needed. Reflection teaches us to learn from our mistakes and to take a closer look at one's own behavior and builds self-regulation and modulation within your student's activities. Breathing, mindfulness, and calm and controlled occupants make for a classroom environment that reflects the same. Levity has its place, as the children love to tell jokes and funny stories. This creates a sense of happiness for all who work and play in the room.

The teacher should use the "ECERS–R, PCMI, SELA Rating Scale" to reflect upon changes that may need to be made to ensure an environment that is safe, secure, and conducive to learning.

Rules: You want to impart character education values through your positive rules. You will be instilling in the students, the development of self-control, as well as self-regulation. Mistakes are accepted as learning experiences. The teacher should never raise her voice, exhibit anger, or use sarcasm or demeaning statements to gain control. You do not want your classroom to reflect negative energy. Your positive outlook will reign supreme.

Regulation: Teachers should model the self-regulation process whenever possible, so students understand that they are learning it. Once you begin this process, you will see the change of atmosphere in the classroom, and when all stakeholders have mastered it, the classroom will become very positive and will be a wonderful place to learn.

Classroom activities that use routines and rituals are critical for alleviating the unpredictable nature of living with adversity. This process helps students to reclaim normalcy and control by supporting a downshift from a fearful state to a calmer and more positive one. Instituting routines and well-orchestrated transitions helps the special needs child, as well as her normal-developing peer, find familiarity in the school day. Posting exemplars of expectations on the wall, role modeling expected behaviors, and rewarding with true praise enable the child to regulate behaviors, setting a positive tone for the climate.

Rubrics: Rubrics allow the children to reflect upon their own learning, as well as acting as a valuable reflection tool. Reflection is the key to regulation. Through rubrics, the child will gain feedback needed to monitor her own progress and make changes. The child will view a task, check the rubric for numerical equivalencies, and work to completion. As soon as the child feels that she has completed the task, she will recheck the rubric posted in the classroom. Upon viewing her score, she can then reflect as to whether she should make adjustments or improvements to her task/objective. She will evaluate and discuss with the teacher when necessary. Rubrics develop independence, and independence leads to a well-run academic climate in the classroom.

When children are confident in emotional, social, and cognitive areas of the curriculum, they contribute to the establishment of a positive classroom. All classrooms should implement the use of behavior and academic rubrics.

SUMMARY

This chapter has comprehensively presented the key components you will need to create a positive environment in your classroom. As an educator, you will begin or continue to implement *The Student Empowerment Program* and all of its components until your classroom reflects a positive atmosphere. Don't give up. If you need to breathe, do so and start fresh. Develop a rapport with the children, and you will gain an understanding of the "nature of the learner" as it plays a crucial part in the development of the positive connections for the next 10 months or longer. Build foundations strong in character education and formulate lessons of interest. Community relationship building aids in the development of a natural learning environment. Your positive environment will exist on its own as a working machine when all components are in place. All who work and play here will have a place and a responsibility to self and others. A safe and open classroom is conducive to learning where collaboration, communication, critical thinking, and creativity abound. Your controlled posture, demeanor, and supportive attitude toward the students provide for regulation and steadfast learning.

The comfort level of the teacher will be accepting; she is one who exhibits tolerance of differences. She is one who views each child as a part of a whole community within the classroom. In addition, your students' experiences in the classroom, like that of Student M and his honest naivete, will expose the underlying presence of the qualities you have worked so hard to develop. As classroom teachers, we build successes indirectly and facilitate the learning that allows freedom to learn and provides an optimum learning experience.

This cooking pot is one that is made up of many ingredients. All of the ingredients are healthy and are equally as important as their counterparts. Combined, these ingredients make a soup that you can "positively" state is the best it can be, as you are the originator of the recipe for a positive classroom environment.

Chapter Four

Play and Exploration and the Early Childhood Learning Brain

Play is the work of a child.

—Maria Montessori

FOCUS OF THE CHAPTER

In this chapter, we will discuss the definition and benefits of play and exploration in early childhood, as well as examine the different types of play children encounter as they go through their stages of development. We will analyze why play and exploration are imperative to the learning brain model. In addition, we will show how the teacher will use *The Student Empowerment Program* to promote positive behavior, both structured and unstructured, self-regulation, and student self-modulation during play and exploration.

The Student Empowerment Program and its relationship to play are examined through Dr. Marion Diamond's famous research study using rats, play, and brain development. The stages of play and exploration will be addressed, so that the teacher may incorporate open-ended play in the early childhood classroom and completely comprehend the importance of allowing children the opportunity to play and explore.

FOCUS QUESTIONS FOR THE CHAPTER

1. What is play and exploration?
2. How are play and exploration important to early childhood development?
3. What are the stages of play?
4. What is open-ended play?
5. What do students learn in play and exploration?
6. What do teachers need to understand when implementing an open-ended free playtime?
7. What do administrators need to know when evaluating teachers at work in an open-ended free-play situation?

BACKGROUND

The word *play* is simply defined as engaging in an enjoyable activity at any age level. The word *exploration* means the examination and inquiry of an event or particular situation. When combined, the two words result in the investigation that children (teens and adults too) exhibit while involved in an activity that creates a pleasure for them, an activity that is not stressful.

Many years ago, play was a time provided for the child by parents when the parents needed to get tasks accomplished. Children were sent off to "go play" and told to return before dinner. Today, we know that play is actually a purposeful part of the day and the basis for cognitive, social, and emotional learning.

As Maria Montessori and later Jean Piaget stated, "play is the work of the child," and it is through play and exploration that children learn and make sense of the world in which they live. We must provide children the opportunity to make choices and choose activities in which they can be actively engaged. Play serves the purpose of releasing energy for the child. It allows the child to experience situations. It promotes self-regulation of behavior and facilitates the development of social skills. Children may play alone or with others, but no matter which, it is the firsthand engagement and the overall experience that is so valuable. It is the unstructured and sometimes structured environment that enables the child to learn.

A FAMOUS RESEARCH STUDY ABOUT PLAY AND THE BRAIN: DR. MARION DIAMOND

In 1964, researchers examined the brains of rats and watched how they played. What the researchers discovered led parents and educators to a totally new mindset about teaching and learning in early childhood education.

Dr. Marion Diamond of the University of California, Berkeley and her colleagues provided the world with a landmark case regarding brain development in rats. They discovered that rats who were raised in poor, diminished environments and were subjected to boring, solitary confinement had smaller and thinner cerebral cortexes than rats raised in fertile and enriched environments that were filled with toys and tunnels to explore. In subsequent analysis of the same, the research team was able to confirm its original findings, with no changes in the original data. Rats who were allowed to play had bigger brains and were smarter. These rats found their way through mazes by using cause-and-effect methods.

WHAT IMPACT DOES THIS RESEARCH HAVE ON EARLY CHILDHOOD EDUCATION?

Play impacts the brain in humans by causing the prefrontal cortex to become bigger, faster. The act of playing changes the connections of the neurons at the front of a human's brain. When the old adage "use it or lose it" is applied, our neural connections become stronger and faster. It's like driving to a familiar place; we feel comfortable driving to a place in which we are familiar and can go there quite quickly. This is not necessarily true if we want to go to an unfamiliar place. The unfamiliarity may cause us to be more cautious and slower in our driving methods.

The brain of the young child is developing rapidly and preparing to go through experiences in play and exploration in order to develop a sense of self, responsibility, and socially acceptable behavior and learn to work collaboratively.

Play and exploration are important because it is here in the prefrontal cortex that emotions, planning, skill building, and problem solving are developed. Children need to be exposed to free, open-ended play to make the most of their brain development and learning.

OPEN-ENDED FREE PLAY: WHAT IS IT?

Open-ended, freedom of expression, spontaneity, inquiry, self-confidence, adventurous, meaningful, communicative, collaborative, and *involved* are words that can be used to describe the act of open-ended free play and exploration. Although all of these words are similar in their perception as they relate to play, the two words that are the most influential in the list are *open ended*.

Open-ended play are the words that are understood by most early childhood educators as the ones that allow for optimal brain development and that make the most gains in cognitive, social, and emotional skill building. This is because open-ended play promotes metacognition and facilitates sense and meaning for the child in a social setting. Open-ended, or free, play provides for limitless possibilities and a natural inclination for using manipulatives, materials, and supplies. The process is twofold as the child's brain has the natural inclination to investigate, but the materials must also be developmentally appropriate to stimulate the brain to use them. The teacher must establish the latter in order for the environment to be conducive for exploration and play.

The brain will react and extend play into new areas. When a child is involved in free play, he makes up his own rules and expectations and uses his own creativity to develop the play as he wants. In other words, there is no adult intervention about how to play "correctly."

While children are playing, *The Student Empowerment Program* is in effect and although there are no rules or adult intervention in the actual play, the stages of the program are in place. The result is positive, socially acceptable behavior; character education values; self-reflection; and self-regulation, all demonstrated by the children.

Are you familiar with the cliché "the process is more important than the endpoint or goal?" Or maybe you remember "it's the process, not the product."

IT'S THE PROCESS

Oftentimes, teachers will recite these quotes when the parents are gathered, explaining to them that they will be receiving a (art) product. They continue to point out that it will be sent home every three days or so. Some parents may need to better comprehend those statements. The parents may think that each product requires a grade, but to the early childhood educator, it clearly does not. The exploration and process are all that are necessary. The product is the end goal of a process that requires freedom of expression and creativity. When a parent or teacher precuts shapes and does part of the "art project" for the learner, we know this is not beneficial.

Some teachers will want *all* the children to complete *their* projects. This may be the main reason it takes so long to send the product home. It may require three days for that teacher to have all 24 children complete it. In essence, the truth is that the three days of time may be required for the children to fully enjoy the work that they are doing, such as tearing and gluing by themselves, no matter how the end product appears when done.

When applying the two quotes to the early childhood learner, one must remember that the child may choose to do the art project or not. Some teachers fret that they will not learn the skills and objectives. Realistically, that skill will be repeated elsewhere at a different center, at some other time, and that child will complete that objective. A master teacher will make a note of this skill and make sure the child attempts the skill on his time and place. The important thing to remember is that we want children to become independent learners and to challenge themselves and take part in their learning. Hence, they need to be challenged and learn self-regulation strategies. (Note: It's important to model numbers and letters for correction formation, but not artwork.)

It's important for administrators to understand that, even though a project may require three days for a child to finish an art project or 30 days to finish a Project Approach model, it *is* executive functioning that the teacher will be addressing while she is facilitating the students. Michelangelo didn't complete the Sistine Chapel in 2.5 hours (the length of a half-day prekindergarten class). An administrator must keep this in mind while evaluating. The administrator must realize that it is the teacher who allows for continuation, creativity, and the self-regulation of the child, and therefore it is the teacher who should receive the highest scores in her evaluation.

With the onset of Universal Prekindergarten, it would be highly recommended for all stakeholders, especially administrators, to refresh or newly educate themselves about early childhood education. Everyone involved should have a strong knowledge base of development and understand the hows and whys of working with early childhood students. Without this knowledge, administrators may give a poor report regarding teachers who are allowing children to have a 45-minute block of time for free play.

A 45- to 60-minute amount of time allows the child who is playing in an open-ended manner the ability to plan, implement, evaluate, and change her activity. The long period of time will allow for the child to engage in the activity and interact with her peers. A shorter amount of time does not allow the brain to scaffold the learning to a greater place. A large amount of space is needed for play as well, and a wide range of quality materials based on developmental levels, interests, and learning styles should be supplied. This is the responsibility of the teacher.

An open-ended classroom has an abundance of materials to spark the child's interest, stimulate the imagination, and engage the child in real and make-believe play. Materials should be left purposefully in the centers with simple instructions if needed. A designated area can be arranged with ongoing projects. To increase independence and self-regulation, the child is in charge of reclaiming his piece and putting the finishing touches on it to bring closure to his work.

AN EXAMPLE OF OPEN-ENDED PLAY

A child playing with a LEGO set, for instance, may have a long-term goal enabling her to continue her engagement in her interest area, as well as the play that enables her to learn math, science, engineering, technology, communication skills, cooperative skills, and fine motor skills. LEGO play requires planning and organizing in the brain, as well as carrying out the daily learning targets. These small, interlocking blocks allow the child to play and explore without the fear of failure. It is a pressureless activity, as are all open-ended free-play situations.

THE TEACHER'S ROLE

During the 45 to 60 minutes of free play for the students, the teacher will be conducting her lessons. There are days when you will assess children by observing and taking anecdotal notes in open-ended free play. Other days you may assess the students by observation and review their data collection at centers (for example, you taught "sink and float" in science, and now you have a sink-and-float table available during free play).

You will observe the child using the area correctly or not and placing the item in the correct category, such as boats under the float title and rocks under the sink title, on the waterproof mat. A follow-up data sheet was introduced at center time, so that the children could draw and record the number of items that sank and the number that floated. At the same time, during the free-play time, you will also be teaching a new lesson, which is associated with the interests of the children.

If this week, during center time, the children came to a unanimous decision to add outer space to the free-play area, you as the teacher can provide a refrigerator box, aluminum foil, helmets, space costumes, boots, walkie-talkies, string, space music compact disc, crayons in neon colors, stickers, colored paper, cardboard tubes, books on space travel, and so forth.

You will observe that during free-play time, the children are utilizing the materials on their own by investigation, and, not so surprisingly, they are doing so prior to the teacher's lesson on outer space. This is because some children have prior knowledge of the Earth, as well as outer space and the solar system, and are creating meaning for the others who are now interested and have begun learning (see the lesson on outer space in chapter 6).

The teacher is also noting those items in *The Student Empowerment Program* that need tweaking in the classroom, so that she can help facilitate positive interactions, communication, collaboration, critical thinking, and creativity.

FACILITATING PLAY

As a master teacher, you will want to facilitate this open-ended exploration by helping the children increase their independence and acknowledge their strengths and weaknesses through multiple tasks and help them to communicate and make real-world connections. As a teacher of a classroom, you will want to "just watch" and collect anecdotal data of your prodigies as they grow socially, intellectually, emotionally, creatively, physically, linguistically, and spiritually.

You will want to be the facilitator of the whole child, using all the learning modalities and applying skills in real-world activities. You will want to encourage learning through hands-on activities in your classroom. The key to the child's success and your ability to become a well-rounded early childhood teacher is based on whether or not you can allow for unstructured play in the classroom. It's not an easy task to not interfere; your mindset will have to be strong and secure and allow the classroom machine to work on its own.

Fun and learning come from open-ended play, which has the best effect on overall development and learning of the child. Refrain from imposing yourself into the play because it will not produce the same results and most definitely destroys the work of the child.

RULES OF PLAY

Play should last a minimum of 45 minutes in a 180-minute program. Of that time, the full 45 minutes should be dedicated to indoor play and an additional 30 minutes to outdoor play. The play in this chapter does not include technology play. No matter whether you teach prekindergarten or 3rd grade, play and exploration *are a one-size-fits-all* activity. Fun-filled play to learn is the same for all children. Play that begins in prekindergarten and continues during the early childhood years enables children to develop fine and gross motor skills and language and socialization skills; scaffolds their learning; develops self-regulation skills, reflective techniques, and motor planning; and helps them understand emotions and feelings and solve problems.

It is important to know the types of play, so you can better understand the developmental levels and nature of your learners.

TYPES OF PLAY

While you read the following list, please keep an open mind; think of the developmental levels of children and attempt to visualize a prekindergarten classroom and 1st-, 2nd-, and 3rd-grade classrooms filled with students ranging in ages from three to eight. Let go of the role of teacher for a moment, and think about how play evolves as you look at the list. Maybe you are presently in a classroom or a caretaker of children or have your own children. In your mind's eye, concentrate on how unstructured play has affected the whole child that you know. Did you allow it to exist, and did you allow the children to explore and inquire? Was your experience with play self-directed or teacher directed? Certain types of play are associated, but are not restricted to specific age groups. Adults play as well as children, although the focus of this book is on early childhood play.

There are many types of play. Table 4.1 describes them. The last three types on this list would lend themselves to older children, unless they were exposed to circumstances.

Table 4.1. Types of Play

Unoccupied play	Birth to 3 months: An infant is busy making random movements and sounds with no clear purpose. This is the first sign of play.
Solitary play and symbolic play	About 3–18 months: Toddler to 6 yrs. and adulthood: Babies will begin playing on their own. They are engaged in their own play and may not notice others playing nearby. They expand their universe by touching, grabbing, mouthing, and rattling objects.
Outdoor play	Toddler years: Children observe other children at play. They are learning how to relate to others, as well as communicating through quickly advancing language development. Outdoor play lends itself to some early partner or group play.
Parallel play	About 18 months to 2 years: Children play alongside each other without any interaction. Some words emerge, but if not met with equal play and intelligence, the other child will not respond.
Associative play	About 3 years: Children are interested in watching other children more than in their toys. During this loosely organized play, children are learning to socialize with peers. Rules are not yet formed, but the dos and don'ts of playing together are learned. This is a very intellectual stage, as it teaches sharing, language development, problem solving, and cooperation. Children at this age share similar goals.
Social play and pretend play	About ages 3–4: Social skills are being learned. Toys and games are shared. Exercise and muscle strength are developing. Children learn to take turns, and it doesn't matter whether they win or lose during this play. Children are pretending from their own experiences, like cooking in the kitchen with daddy, and can sequence the events of the experience. Children have the ability to show cause and effect.
Motor–physical play	About 2–3 years: Children can now run, jump, hop, throw, and catch with large balls. They can push themselves with their feet on a riding toy. They will freely give up their toy to share with another child, and it still doesn't matter whether they win or lose at a game.
Constructive play	About 2 years of age, when the attention span is longer: Children will begin to create things, build towers, knock them down and rebuild them again, play in sand and water, and use clay-dough. They like drawing and painting. Children take pride in accomplishments. They like numbers and concepts and gain confidence.

Expressive play	Emerging at 3–4 and advancing: Children learn to express feelings. Materials may include paints, crayons, colored pencils, chalk, and markers for drawing and writing. Children may invite adults to take an active role in the expressive play and interact with them about feelings and creativity.
Fantasy and advanced dramatic play	5–6 years: Children are now playing in multiple roles, such as the mother, big sister, baby, doctor, or police officer. Play includes highly imaginative themes with multiple plans and sequences. Language is being used to the set scene and includes understanding and use of inference skills, predicting, and nonverbal communication, such as gestures and body and facial expressions. Imagination is strong.
Cooperative play	About 4 or later in preschool year: This play is organized and has group goals developed and enforced by the participants themselves. Rules are now in force, and feelings can be hurt easily, as children are either in or out of a group. Children move from a self-centered world to a world of social interactions.
Recapitulative play	Allows children to explore history, rituals, stories, rhymes, fire, and darkness.
Rough-and-tumble play	Play that is certainly physical, but has less to do with fighting and more to do with touching, tickling, and gauging relative strength.
Deep play	Allows children to encounter risky or even potentially life-threatening experiences, to develop survival skills and conquer fear.

A REAL-LIFE PLAY EXPERIENCE

Imagine you are in a kindergarten classroom and are observing a child dressed in an apron in the housekeeping area, ready to cook. She is singing a song that her father sings when making soup. She is adding plastic vegetables, fruit, and pretend cans of food, while diligently stirring the soup (adults know there is no water or stock in this soup base, but she does not).

The second child, who is in the block center, is stacking square rubber blocks. He is positioning them, so that he can build a high tower. When he gets all eight blocks in place, he decides to add a flat-based, triangular rubber ring to the very top as a roof.

The second child decides that he needs to reduce the size of the block tower and tries again. This time, it works and he says, "Look! If I only build this high, I can put the roof on the house."

These children are playing during free play and are exploring their surroundings, using fine and gross motor skills, spatial relationships, and language skills. They are both on task and are working through a sequence of events in their own minds.

Educationally, we are aware that there are two different theories happening in this vignette. It is apparent to us that the first is simply the child reenacting what she already knows. It would be safe to assume that one of her parents wears an apron when he or she cooks and, while cooking, sings this familiar tune that the child has repeated. This child has used previously learned skills and knowledge, but has not introduced any new knowledge or skills into the play encounter. She has no knowledge that soup cannot have cans in it or that it requires some type of liquid. She has observed this in her household, but has not learned everything she needs to know yet.

The other child has chosen familiar rubber blocks and, through his cognitive development, has discovered he made a judgment error while building. He can rectify the problem on his own. He is problem solving. He chooses a random but deliberate action to reduce the number of squares in his tower, in hopes that the triangular ring will stay balanced on the roof of his shorter building. It does.

The role of the teacher in both of these situations is different. After observing the soup-making child, the teacher will make a mental or written note to make soup in class, specifically highlighting for this child the parts that she needs to learn. Or the teacher may join the play in hopes that her presence brings another child over who says "We need to add water." At this junction, the teacher may say, what is the water for in soup? No interruption of play, just a simple teachable moment. Regarding the tower-building child, the teacher may begin to build a tower out of steadier blocks alongside him and, without interrupting the play, hope that he takes notice and either joins or begins to "borrow" her blocks for himself.

WHAT CHILDREN LEARN IN PLAY

Table 4.2 is a chart of cognitive skills that are learned when the child is allowed to discover and explore the following areas of learning. This chart is not limited to these areas or these specific learned skills, as there are many more. Many of the areas overlap and, of course, skills are learned in more than one area. Cross-curricular activities within the early childhood classroom are very important. For example, it's important to have blocks in the dramatic play area if you need to make steps for your house.

Table 4.2. Cognitive Skills Learned in Types of Play

Block play	Motor planning, fine and gross motor skills, mathematics including measurement, comparison, number operations, estimation, symmetry, geometry, spatial reasoning, scientific reasoning, hypothesis, attention span, social skills, and self-esteem
Dramatic play	Self-regulation, self-modulation, emotional support or outlet for emotions, conflict resolution, problem solving in groups, literacy and language development, gross and fine motor coordination, creativity, formulation of new ideas, use of knowledge to expand actions, sequencing, social skills
Water and sand play	Math, science, sinking and floating, changing of state, sensory experiences, physics, chemistry, math, biology (by adding other things to water play), fine motor, language and concept development such as scoop, sift, pour, dig, tunnel, eye–hand coordination, social skills, venting emotions like anger, stress relief, calming, breathing techniques as well as self-control
Science exploration	Exploration, discovery, inventiveness, imagination, fine and gross motor control, chemical and physical changes, hypothesis, estimation, attention to details, problem solving, reasoning, properties, classification, predictions, questioning
Math exploration	Thinking and reasoning, questioning, patience, approaching answers in different ways, critical thinking, classifying, patterns, shapes, spatial relations, enumerating, exploration of taking apart and putting together objects, directionality, symmetry, mathematical foundation building, academic achievement
Reading readiness	Practice makes perfect (a reader may take a book to the beanbag chair to read to the class), critical thinking, concentration, attention span, eye–hand coordination, sequencing, comprehension, literacy development, learning in the real world, vocabulary, enjoyment, empathy, tolerance, patience, leadership, social skills, academic achievement
Music discovery	Rhythm, patterns, sound likes and dislikes, self-worth, listening, hearing, singing, attention span, increases in mathematical abilities, vibrations, scientific principles, self-discipline, self-regulation, self-modulation, social skills, patience, counting, beat, tones, delayed gratification, perseverance, memorization, culture, self-esteem, challenge, sensory experiences, calm
Art discovery	Creativity, imagination, problem solving, sensory experiences, nonverbal communication via the art medium, patience, perseverance, disappointment, happiness, calm, emotions, understanding and accepting constructive feedback, collaboration, preparedness, dedication, focus, concentration

SUMMARY

Children who are allowed to play and explore will flourish in their lives and have the ability to use many higher-order thinking skills, as well as problem-solving skills. Knowledge of how play develops and what stages children are in during play are two of the most important things a teacher should know before executing a classroom with play and exploration.

Administrators should have a keen awareness of why their early childhood teacher facilitates as she does for the student. Understanding the nature of the learner, the developmental level of the student, and the stages of play, as well as the learning outcomes from play and exploration, is of the utmost concern of the adults in the classroom. If left to random choice, the experience may be dull and uninviting. By allowing children a large space and a large block of time, with fun-filled, challenging, creative, and high-quality materials, the teacher is setting the stage for a quality early childhood experience.

Chapter Five

Lesson Design and the Early Childhood Learning Brain

FOCUS OF THE CHAPTER

In this chapter we will discuss how to design a lesson, with the nature of the learner in mind. Common Core State Standards, as well as the Early Childhood Learning Standards, which are critical components to daily lessons, are addressed in this chapter. Project-based learning in early childhood education and the attributes of lesson design and lesson delivery, using the Learner's Brain Model, are considered. In addition, we will address how to deliver lessons that are student centered and that promote self-regulation and encourage positive behavior management.

FOCUS QUESTIONS FOR THE CHAPTER

1. How do I plan a lesson using early childhood brain research and the nature of the learner?
2. What format should I use for my lesson design?
3. Why should my lessons be standards based?
4. What standards should I follow?
5. What are the implications for lesson design and teaching?
6. What is the Project Approach to learning?
7. What is Universal Prekindergarten in the United States?
8. How does video gaming teach me about lesson design?

BACKGROUND

As a teacher, you may be required to incorporate brain research into your lesson design, as well as provide differentiated instruction to the students. This chapter will address the changes in the formats of lesson designs over the years and will help you to learn how to design a quality lesson, with the *nature of the learner* in mind. A review of the Common Core State Standards, as well as the Early Childhood Learning Standards, will be considered because they are critical components to daily lessons. Early childhood teachers, as well as upper grade–level teachers, will marvel in the Project Approach to learning and its relevance to the students' success in the classroom.

After reading this chapter, it will become apparent that writing a lesson is not about copying from the teacher's guide in science, math, reading, or social studies; it is about creating sense and meaning for the student through readiness sets, instructional delivery, essential questions, objectives, goals, reasoning, problem-solving and relationships skills, and conclusions based on a student's strengths and weaknesses.

START WITH STANDARDS

Many districts have a curriculum that is standards based, which are developed by companies who claim to understand the nature of the learner. In addition to your district's preformatted curriculum standards, an early childhood educator should employ the standards put forth by the National Association for the Education of Young Children (NAEYC). You will want to use the standards set forth by your district (many districts use the NAEYC standards in early childhood education), but it is also imperative for early childhood educators to use the lessons based on the 10 standards from the NAEYC. Through these standards, the teacher will find it easy to remain cognizant of the developmental level of the children, provide lessons that are multicultural and differentiated, use exploration and play in lessons, create small- and large-group interactions, and design lessons that are developmentally appropriate based on brain research. The NAEYC has improved the quality of early learning programs for young children over the decades. It is also an excellent resource for teachers, as their website offers tools and resources for successful learning opportunities.

Currently, you will find many districts implementing these standards and requiring prekindergarten and kindergarten teachers to use the NAEYC standards numerical listings, instead of the Common Core State Standards (CCSS).

COMMON CORE STATE STANDARDS (CCSS)

If you were not in a teaching position in the year 2009, you may be using the Common Core State Standards without a true knowledge of the whys and wherefores. These standards are crucial components of your lesson, as they set the expectations for your planning.

The state-led effort to develop the CCSS began in 2009 by state leaders, governors, and state commissioners of education. They recognized the value of uniform standards, which related to real-world learning goals. These standards were formulated to ensure students graduating from high school would be prepared for higher education, careers, and life.

These expectations were outlined for teachers, and teachers are now required to list them as part of their daily lesson plan. Many teachers wondered and stressed over how they were going to be able to incorporate all of these standards into a daily lesson plan. Many years ago, teachers would plan lessons that *they knew* met the needs of their students. They were familiar with what they had been using and didn't want to make a change. They believed *they knew* the nature of their learners well enough to create lessons without standards. When the new standards were presented, they asked why changes were necessary. In actuality, teachers did reach the goals they set for their students by *just knowing* what they needed, but were required to incorporate the standards anyway. A master teacher knows the child well, and, coupled with the new standards, it was only a win-win situation for the student.

PRESCHOOL TEACHING AND LEARNING STANDARDS

The most required and influential document for preschool education and one that aligns itself with the NAEYC standards and the CCSS is the Preschool Teaching and Learning Standards. This framework of standards delivers high-quality educational experiences to preschool learners. The theoretical bases lie in the supportive learning environment, guidance, and developmentally appropriate assessment of skills and checklists of skills for learning outcomes. In addition, it advocates for a strong home/school connection between families and community members. The standards serve as best practice guidelines for what teachers must know about the nature of the learner to provide and promote positive social, emotional, and cognitive experiences for the students now and in their future. It seeks to optimize learning and development, so that the children will have long-lasting effects in their lives.

NAEYC STANDARDS, PRESCHOOL TEACHING AND LEARNING STANDARDS, AND CCSS AND LESSON PLANNING

The NAEYC Standards, Preschool Teaching and Learning Standards, and CCSS are easily understood by all stakeholders in early childhood education. Each of the standards describes characteristics that, when intertwined with each other and used in a best practice manner, provide the stakeholders (teachers, support staff, and administrators) the opportunity to create quality lessons in an early childhood learning program.

Based on this knowledge, teachers are able to use the information to plan lesson goals and student learning targets (objectives.) All of the standards help to make teachers more knowledgeable about the nature of their learners. One should integrate the standards and keep in mind the complexities of the families, community, and students. By formulating lessons with the integration of curriculum district standards, NAEYC Standards, Preschool Teaching and Learning Standards, and the CCSS, you will be mindful of each child's uniqueness. As a teacher, by implementing these standards, you are building the foundation for your teaching pedagogy, and you will be able to implement this knowledge when planning your lessons. It is apparent that the child's learning is first and foremost, as well as how to accomplish this through the standards goals. The nature of the learner is highly important and should be considered when writing lessons.

UNIVERSAL PREKINDERGARTEN: A NEW INITIATIVE

Universal Prekindergarten is a new initiative in the United States. Early childhood advocates believe that a quality education program should be available for four-year-old students, providing they are eligible. Eligibility is left up to the individual states and is similar to kindergarten criteria for the state. Many professionals feel early learning will increase test scores in the future by providing a strong cognitive, social, and emotional beginning for the young learner. Teachers who are being selected for the program will need to follow standards of curriculum that are closely related to kindergarten curricula, but all states have the ability to pick and choose their own method of teaching.

A KINDERGARTEN EXAMPLE OF IMPLEMENTING NAEYC STANDARDS

When planning a lesson for kindergarten children, you will find standards from the NAEYC that address relationships, curriculum, teaching, assessment of child progress, health, staff competencies, families, community relationships, physical environment, leadership, and management. In addition to keeping the standards in mind for the development of the lesson, the teacher should also be aware of the developmental level of the child, the child's strengths and weaknesses, the use of exploration and play in the lesson design, the incorporation of small- and large-group interactions, provide for a sufficient amount of child-directed hands-on activities, develop a child's higher-level thinking skills and goal development, provide time for planning, hypothesizing, and query in the lesson, and so much more. It is obvious that balance is the key to an exemplary lesson in all grades. Without standards, lesson planning would be random and at the discretion of each teacher, and assessment would not qualify as equal and fair for all children.

LESSON PLAN DESIGN IN THE BEGINNING

What did our lesson design look like in the past, and how has it changed over the decades? As a teacher, you may or may not remember "writing lesson plans" in your daily lesson planner each week, or maybe a few of you are still scripting by hand. As far back as one can remember, teachers were taught to list subjects, times, dates, and pages of class work and homework in daily lesson books. Today, in the "age of technology" and advancements in computers, teachers are entering data and devising templates to design lessons, thereby simplifying lesson development.

Initially, plan books contained rectangular or square boxes that looked a lot like a graph. They were sectioned by weeks, with the days across the top or down one side. Weekly objectives were listed at the top of the page. Teachers listed the special activities, events, and the core standards in these boxes, with any other pertinent information, such as the initials of the children who needed extra help or the disabilities of special needs children, as it related to the lesson.

The lesson plan merely consisted of a few items: Title of the Lesson, Objective, and Length of the Lesson, Core Curriculum State Standards (i.e., CCSS.ELA-LITERACY.RH.6-8.2), Materials, Procedure, and Conclusion.

The plan book was given to the substitute in the teacher's absence and was also used for the teacher as a daily reminder of his schedule. Lesson plans were sometimes "suggestive" in that they were used randomly, even though they were done at the request of the principal or supervisor. New teachers had to show their knowledge of the subject matter in their plan books. More often, a written lesson was not always required as long as one showed his or her schedule in the plan book. This, of course, was also based upon your district, as there were districts that required them more often.

Today's lesson planning is completed on the computer and is composed of Title, Standards, Essential Question, Student Learning Target (Objectives), Demonstration of Student Leaning (DSL), Readiness Set, Instructional Activities, Consolidation for Closure, and Reflection.

TEACHING TO THE YOUNG CHILD'S BRAIN: WHAT ARE THE IMPLICATIONS FOR LESSON DESIGN AND TEACHING?

The need for early childhood education (ages two to four) is important because children are born with an estimated 12 to 15 billion nerve cells (called neurons). Each neuron interacts with others by extending branches (called dendrites). Brain researchers have found that the number of synapses per unit volume of tissue (called synaptic density) changes over a person's life span. So, if an infant is born with more brain cells than he or she will need, then by age four, the synaptic densities will be 50% more than that of an adult level. Those neurons that are not used are "pruned." Neurons that are used will link together and form neural networks. After enough repletion, the network connects at a fast rate, and the action is expedited. Every sports coach understands this and must practice, practice, practice, so skills become second nature for their athletes. Or, as a favorite trombone teacher once expressed, "practice slow to go fast." The slow practice reinforces correct skill development and neuronal mapping until it becomes automatic.

TEACHING TO THE YOUNG CHILD'S BRAIN: WHAT ARE THE IMPLICATIONS FOR TEACHING?

Understanding that there are growth cycles for the brain is important for the teacher. Initially, the concept of growth was the notion of development as sequential stages (like the rungs of a ladder). However, we now know that the brain has "plasticity" and grows neurons and makes connections as the student is stimulated in a rich environment. These connections form neural networks, and the process of mind mapping develops. Mind mapping is the ability to build new ideas and make connections or branch off into different areas, from one thought or concept.

In essence, the old notion of conceptual thinking in a progression is replaced with a "dynamic skills framework," which is flexible. Neural networks develop as the neurons make connections. Think of a mind map and how everything is connected. This concept is important for teachers to understand; just learning facts will get the information stored in various parts of the brain, but add a practical application, and then unification of facts in the brain comes together.

This concept has implications for the classroom teacher when planning centers and providing activities and tasks that promote metacognition. The teacher should also incorporate practical activities, so students will see the relationship of what they are learning and how it applies to the objective.

More importantly, the early childhood educator must know the stages of brain growth so appropriate activities can be planned in a developmentally appropriate way.

CONNECTING BRAIN RESEARCH AND EARLY CHILDHOOD TEACHERS

1. Teachers should keep in mind the cyclical nature of cortical growth and optimal cognitive development by providing a rich and rewarding environment.
2. Brain development involves a recurring growth cycle of neural networks and learning. Just teaching facts will get competency, but having hands-on, interactive learning centers and activities for students to apply their knowledge develops neural networks and mind mapping and proficiency.
3. Understanding cognitive growth means understanding that early childhood students can increase brain function and, if a student has not mastered a skill set at a certain point, he or she will still have the opportunity to do so, with or without guidance.
4. Providing a rich and rewarding learning environment and not imposing the knowledge, methods, and content inconsistently with skill acquisition, at the appropriate age level for comprehension, will yield successes.

USING A HANDS-ON APPROACH

The hands-on approach to learning in lesson planning is essential. Developing sense and meaning of a subject is how the brain transfers the learned knowledge to long-term storage. This is best accomplished with hands-on learning and application of skills and concepts. The Project Approach to teaching and learning (also known as project-based learning) is an extremely valuable tool for the teacher. The Project Approach can be suited to any grade level and with any developmental level of student and is widely used with special needs students since it allows for child-directed exploration. It is an integrated and interdisciplinary type of instructional lesson.

Here is how the Project Approach to learning works: The teacher conceives of a project that can be used for students to apply skills they have learned, so it becomes in essence, a performance assessment. It can be literary work, a mathematical model, or an engineering design. The teacher backward designs (starting with the goal or the end point) lessons and provides the necessary skills, which the students need to learn. Boundaries and deadlines are discussed with the students, and the teacher becomes an integral part of the learning. The students organize their tasks and find resources to support their goal. It is the teacher who guides, facilitates, and helps the students figure out the steps in creating their project. The teacher will offer continual feedback to the students during the experience. At the end of their project, the students display and discuss the way they calculated each step of their process and their final outcome.

PROJECT APPROACH NINE-STEP PROCESS

There is a sequence of nine steps when developing project-based learning. Modifications and accommodations are acceptable if the teacher feels that they are appropriate. According to the Association of Supervision and Curriculum Development, in the article titled "Teachers as Classroom Coaches" by Andi Stix and Frank Hrbek, the authors note that:

1. The teacher-coach develops readiness for the lesson by providing students with real-life samples of projects they will be doing.
2. Students assume a role of project designers, so they can start to think like an "expert."
3. Teachers provide students with the necessary skills and knowledge to complete the project, so they will have the competencies to complete the project.
4. The criterion for evaluation of the project is presented, so students can self-regulate their learning.
5. Students accumulate the materials necessary for the project.
6. Students create their projects.
7. Students present their projects.
8. Students reflect on the process.
9. Students evaluate the projects based on the criteria that were established, so they can self-regulate their learning.

The steps are sequential, and a master teacher will decide how to design the lesson based on the nature of the learner using the Learner's Brain Model. Below is a suggested outline of the process.

Step 1: Setting the Stage with the Apple Lesson

A Project Approach–themed lesson was sparked by the donation of 30 apples by a child's parent. The children were interested in the characteristics of the apples and wanted to learn more about apples. First, the students washed them and carefully sliced them with plastic knives, assisted by adults. The teacher began setting the stage for real-life examples. Some of the apples were left whole, and others were categorized by the students into bowls of green, red, and yellow and apples having more than one color on them. The other bowls contained small, medium, and large apples. The sliced apples were placed on paper plates, with a small plastic cup for the collection of seeds. The stems were left intact on some of the slices. A discussion ensued about apples, apple trees, baked goods with apples, the five senses as they relate to apples, and many other subjects to build interest in the students.

Step 2: Project Designers' Roles

The class was divided into groups of three children. The students were assigned tasks to complete based on questions about apples. Teachers and staff kept the questions simple so that the questions were developmentally appropriate for the four- and five-year-old students. The classroom was established to be a resource for the children. There were books, computer sites, real apples, play apples, and supermarket flyers. Phone calls were placed to real farmers, and questions for parents and family members were encouraged. Plasticine and clay-dough, as well as other art projects and cooking projects, were completed with apples as part of the resources for the students. There was discussion about apple studies, and the answers to the questions were provided to the children. Questions included:

- How do apples grow?
- What do we use apples for in our lives?
- What do apples look like on the inside and outside?
- What do apples do for our bodies?
- How does the supermarket get the apples?
- What happens on an apple farm?
- What animals eat apples?

Step 3: Teachers Provide Students with the Necessary Skills and Knowledge

Discussions were informal and held while the students worked.

Step 4: Present Criteria for Evaluation

A rubric is used for this assignment. It is one method that is used a lot in the classroom, and students are very familiar with the process of understanding them. Figure 5.1 is a facsimile of the actual research drawing the team did in answer to their question. All of the team members were responsible for creating a drawing or a writing regarding their findings. Figure 5.2 is the rubric that will be used to evaluate the findings.

Figure 5.1.   Data Picture

My name is _____.

My question is- What do apples look like on the inside and outside? Explain your answer below.

Figure 5.2.   Data Picture

My name is _____.

My question is- *What do apples look like on the inside and outside?*

I found out the answer to my question.	I did not find out the answer to my question.

If you can imagine that the child drew the pictures in the first graph, what would you say about the evaluation? As a teacher using the Project Approach, it is your feedback that will teach the child to move further into the inquiry and research. You may need to eat an apple with the child to further investigate, or you may need to use a book, a field trip on a weekend with the parents, or a call to the farmer for more information. The goal is to answer the question as completely as possible.

Step 5: Accumulating the Necessary Materials

This step was addressed by the teacher, who provided a room full of resources in order to assist the young child with the inquiry.

Step 6: Creating the Project

Encourage the child to use another form of medium after the initial drawing for the rubric. They can use clay, paint, plaster of Paris, templates of apples, material, tissue paper, sponges that resemble the inside of an apple, and real apple seeds to create a project based on the color of the exterior of apples and the interior of apples.

Step 7: Preparing to Present the Project

Incorporate writing for any student who can copy or write such words as *apple*, *seeds*, *red*, *green*, *yellow*, *white*, *spongy*, *crisp*, and *juicy*. They will write or tell where they found the answer to their question and how the team worked together to reach the goal.

Step 8: Presenting the Project

As a group, any child who wishes to tell about what they did may, but no child will be forced to speak.

Step 9: Reflecting on the Process and Evaluating the Project

The project will be compared to the rubric, and the team may discuss how they felt about the question and answer they had to investigate.

In some instances, the Project Approach can be challenging to design lessons, especially if you have a very large class of students. It is a welcome change from the regular routine and with modifications to the format; it can be a motivational tool for the children. Be mindful of the NAEYC Standards,

Preschool Teaching and Learning Standards, and state standards for your curricula when you are formulating goals. Your rubric is your grading requirement for the students, so be cognizant that it allows for the degrees of percentiles in your school's grading system.

Depending on your choice of goals, the project may last anywhere from one to four weeks. Math may be challenging for some children, so this approach is perfect to instill sense and meaning by the use of graphs, charts, and maps. We would encourage every teacher to attempt it to view the actual application of learned knowledge.

A teacher may report that he plans lessons, using the project method and hands-on activities, and he still does not achieve the desired results he was expecting. The answer to this problem lies in the structure of the lesson. A video gamer is a perfect example of how to structure a lesson, so that a student can attend for 40 minutes in class (a video gamer can attend to a game for hours, but 40-minute lessons are most common in schools). Think of the "nature of the gamer."

TEACH LIKE A GAMER

The strategies that video gamers employ in conjunction with a research-based instructional program are found in the Learner's Brain Model. The following strategies will help the teacher plan and implement a model lesson.

The five stages of lesson design are applied and represented by the video-gaming strategies below.

STAGE ONE: THE PLANNING STAGE

Safe Environment

Gamers select *safe environments*. The brains of students in safe, nonthreatening environments are primed to learn the task. The brains of students in threatening, unsafe environments go into survival mode and are primed for one of three actions: fight, flight, or fear. None are conducive to learning.

A safe classroom environment with clear management expectations is necessary for successful teaching. In effective classrooms, teachers create safe environments by establishing rules, protocols, and consequences for inappropriate actions. Teachers act consistently, appropriately, and fairly (master teachers understand fair is not always equal and know how to balance their students' feelings). Students know what to expect, internalize acceptable behavior, and understand the consequences for inappropriate behavior.

Goal Setting

Goal setting is essential when playing video games. Gamers start at one level and use a variety of strategies as they work toward a clearly established goal, achieve the goal, and move onto the next goal. In the instructional setting, when long- and short-term goals are clear and specific, students focus on the lesson.

The Student Learning Target (objective) is the short-term classroom goal; the Essential Question is the long-term goal. The Student Learning Target is the first stage of self-regulation. It provides students with forethought, knowledge, and insight into what is being taught and what they are expected to learn and do. Because the brain needs completeness, knowing the starting and end point (Demonstration of Student Learning, or DSL) enables the brain to see the relationship. Once goals are established, teachers can tier lessons, group students to address individual needs, and post anchor charts to make thinking visible by recording content, strategies, processes, cues, and guidelines during the learning process.

STAGE TWO: INFORMATIONAL STAGE

Achievable Goal

Essential brain mechanisms underlie effective learning. Gamers have the option to resume the previous challenge or to begin a new one. Those who begin a new challenge maintain a sense of confidence and believe that they will be successful. In their mind, the new challenge becomes an *achievable goal*.

Achievable goals ensure success. The brain releases dopamine. Dopamine improves concentration, arouses pleasure, and creates a desire to experience the sensation and its resultant chemical release again. Information concerning the success is stored in the brain. Each success ensures that the storage becomes permanent.

Prior Knowledge

When students set goals, they take ownership of an object, idea, or person. This "endowment effect" ensures that the object becomes integrated within their sense of identity, and it is something they are reluctant to give it up. Couple the endowment effect with the release of dopamine, and the result is incremental successes and students striving to reach their goals. *Prior knowledge* is activated. Students remember what they did to be successful and what they learned to avoid when they were not successful. It is easier to learn something new when one can link it to something already known. A specific part of the brain—the medial prefrontal cortex—is an important part of this process.

STAGE THREE: LESSON DELIVERY

Incremental Progress

Incremental progress is promoted by feedback. Gamers make incremental progress toward achieving the video-game goals and by increasing levels of complexity because video games provide immediate feedback in the form of reward or failure. Such feedback promotes corrective behavior by providing gamers with information and insight into what works.

When students perceive their learning environment as positive and they receive positive supports, endorphins are released, the frontal part of the brain (the executive section) is stimulated, and the learners experience feelings of euphoria. Incremental progress builds on success. This explains why, for example, computerized learning is successful. It is adaptive. Gamers master one level before moving to the next level. Students make incremental progress when teachers differentiate their lessons, give meaningful feedback, and provide students opportunities to proceed at their own level.

Immediate Feedback

Video games are adaptive and provide *immediate feedback* to the gamer. Good choices are rewarded, and the gamer gets to move onto the next level. Bad choices provide learning opportunities and the chance to try again. In a similar way, immediate feedback makes it possible for students to self-correct, self-regulate, and self-monitor their behavior. Neurons make connections during learning and are strengthened by clear goals and positive feedback. Neurons connect with new neurons to form new connections: "Neurons that fire together wire together."

Negative feedback and episodes of failure, on the other hand, drain the brain of dopamine and make it difficult for the learner not only to concentrate but also to learn from what went wrong.

Rewards or Incentives

Video games provide *rewards or incentives* in the form of bonus points or additional "lives." Successful gamers feel a rush of excitement; they are eager to move onto the next challenge. Successes promote a "growth mind-set" as gamers experience incremental success.

The more times learners succeed at something, the longer their brains store the information that supported their success in the first place. With each success, the learner's brain releases dopamine. As dopamine flows into the brain's reward pathway (the part responsible for pleasure, learning, and motivation), not only are students able to concentrate more fully, but they also feel inspired to experience the activity again due to the chemical release. This stimulation process, brain stimulation reward (BRS), reacts and reinforces behaviors, especially if the rewards are tied to a goal.

The Brain Is a Pattern Seeker

Gamers look *for patterns* to help them move from one challenge to the next. Computer games are effective for brain training and have been shown to improve vision, memory, and problem solving. Because memory is a residue of thought, gamers remember what did and did not work.

The brain seeks patterns. Pattern recognition is the ability to consider a complex set of inputs with hundreds of features and make decisions based on a comparison of some component, encountered or learned, of the subset. During the superior pattern processes (SPP), the brain forms "cognitive maps" and begins to look for new patterns. To establish patterns, students must attend to and focus on their surroundings. Activities must be challenging while providing students the opportunities for productive struggle, which ultimately leads to success. There must be a balance between too much and not enough stress. With too much stress, the brain shuts down. With not enough stress, the brain does not attach importance to the task. The key is to cognitively challenge students to struggle productively and to work above their comfort level, which is what gamers do when they play video games at growing levels of complexity.

STAGE FOUR: CONSOLIDATION FOR CLOSURE

How Do I Beat This Level?

When facing difficulties, gamers may check the guidebook to gain insight into how to "beat the level." This usually occurs after they stumble at a difficult level and ponder what they must do to succeed. They self-regulate and reflect on what works and what needs to be changed.

A similar process takes place in successful classrooms. Teachers do this when they conduct a consolidation for closure at the end of a lesson and use that information to adjust the lesson. Students do this when they reflect on the lesson and make necessary adjustments for future assignments. The process of closure enables learners to consolidate information, something that often occurs during sleep, to determine what is important and significant.

STAGE FIVE: REFLECTION

How Did I Do?

Reflection is essential for self-regulated learning. It promotes continuous growth, meaning, and relevancy. Gamers reflect on what they did to be successful. When they do well at one level, they can brag about their success. High scores are posted for everyone to see. Achieving ever more challenging goals is rewarded and builds self-confidence. Posted achievements promote a feeling of pride. Bragging with friends on social media triggers pleasurable sensations in the brain.

Peer teaching is a powerful tool for student growth. It allows students to practice what they learned, as well as strengthen their own neural pathways. Students will help friends who are having difficulties at levels in which they succeeded. They teach their friends what they must do to succeed. Giving learners opportunities to share their knowledge with others promotes students' attention and mental organization during instruction.

Gamers feel good when they win. They look forward to challenges inherent in the next level of play. Students feel good when they succeed at challenging tasks. They take pride in their incremental successes. Dopamine is released in their brains, and they look forward to the next cognitive challenge.

Video games can teach more than how to beat opponents. They can provide educators with strategies to engage learners and to promote student success, all grounded in brain research.

Using strategies of a video gamer and planning hands-on activities consistent with Project Approach learning should yield the desired results.

SUMMARY

Reflecting upon this chapter, one can see how lesson design has evolved over the years. Many years ago, a lesson plan was created mainly for the teacher as a reminder of what he has to accomplish for the day or week. Current lesson plans are highly intricate, easily completed on the computer, tiered to meet the needs of the learner, and brain research based.

This chapter reviewed the components of creating an exemplary lesson with the inclusion of the NAEYC Standards, the Preschool Teaching and Learning Standards, the CCSS, and your own district's standards. The implications for teachers using the standards and practical application of the same were highlighted in the apple lesson plan using the Project Approach to learning. Finally, a comparison of video gaming and lesson design was presented so that the reader would understand that engaging students in a lesson plan is more than just copying objectives from the curriculum guide.

Chapter 6

Assessments and Rubrics and the Early Childhood Learning Brain

FOCUS OF THE CHAPTER

One common type of an assessment is the rubric. It provides a continuum for the students to use in assessing their progress. It also allows the students to self-assess their progress based on established standards, and removes the allegation of prejudice or bias. More importantly, the students can self-assess their progress and self-regulate and self-manage their learning. It is a great tool for student self-regulation.

A rubric is a set of criteria that matches the description of students' work levels of performance. It does not always evaluate the work of the student but more so assesses the performance related to the objective of the work. In this chapter, we will discuss how using rubrics promotes a mindset in the students that allows them to know what is expected of them and to assess their own work, so that they can meet the objective at every level.

Rubrics are an integral part of *The Student Empowerment Program* because they promote student empowerment by allowing the students to take charge of their learning. The students determine what needs to be done to achieve the next level. It also allows the students to become independent learners and seek resources needed to complete the goal.

As you read this chapter, it will become apparent to you as to why we advocate for the use of rubrics in early childhood education. We have provided you with valuable information on rubrics and formal assessments, but ultimately, it will be your decision about which ones you choose to use in your classroom. Finally, we will present you with types of assessments, as well as examples of rubrics. We will correlate the rubrics with the nature of the early childhood learner, a sample lesson, and *The Student Empowerment Program*.

FOCUS QUESTIONS FOR THE CHAPTER

1. What is a rubric?
2. What are the types of rubrics?
3. How are rubrics used to advance student learning?

4. When is it appropriate to use a rubric in an early childhood lesson?
5. How can a student learn self-regulation and become a self-dependent learner by using a rubric?

BACKGROUND

Teachers encourage students to do many things, but how often do you think that using rubrics will promote self-regulation? When a teacher distributes rubrics to his students, based on his objective for a given task, he alters the child's route to learning in a productive, self-regulated way.

When the child learns information from the teacher or parent, it is the responsibility of the adult to ascertain how much information was retained by the child. This degree of retention should be measured in order for the teacher to prepare a strategic goal-setting plan toward the student's continued success. A rubric may be used as a tool to define whether the child has reached her goal. In early childhood education, the rubric is likely to be a process- or product-based instrument, and the assessment of a student's performance is the teacher's and student's responsibility.

The results of this measurement must meet the needs of the early learner, as well as standards required by your state and school district. In early childhood education, we prefer the rubric method of assessment so learners can self-regulate their learning, understand what they need to do to improve, and maintain standards at each level of operation.

THE EARLY CHILDHOOD BRAIN ON RUBRICS

The early childhood brain is complex, and children are learning at rapid rates in school and at home. The goal of the teacher (or parent) is to help the child strive toward self-regulation and success in all that he does. A rubric can assist the child to become an intelligent citizen and lifelong learner. By instilling a sense of success in the learner, the teacher or parent is also developing motivation in the student.

HOW DO WE KNOW WHETHER THE STUDENT IS RETAINING THE INFORMATION?

Observation during work or play is one way a teacher can decide whether the information taught is being applied to new situations. This observation method is very general in nature and leaves areas of learning untouched. The teacher may be indecisive regarding the extent in which the child has actually digested the new knowledge. The teacher may also wonder whether the new knowledge has continued through the neural pathways to long-term memory, been stored, and is retrievable at a later date. What should a teacher do when confronted with this dilemma?

The answer from a teacher's point of view is quite simple: "test 'em." Observations are general, and testing is specific. That is a fact. Testing comes with its downside as well. Tests in the early childhood classroom may be made up of bubble markings, multiple choices, and fill in the blanks. Tests can create anxiety and must be handled correctly, if they are used at all. Creating test anxiety is not a goal of the early childhood teacher, nor any teacher (or parent), for that matter, so developing a fun, self-esteem–building, and independent alternative is what is suggested.

RUBRICS AND ASSESSMENTS

Assessment provides educators, parents, and families with critical information about a child's development and growth. Rubrics provide the student with critical information about his performance. This factor needs to be stressed the most!

WHAT ARE THE DIFFERENT CHILD ASSESSMENT METHODS?

Methods of child assessment can be informal (conducting natural observations, collecting data, and work for portfolios, using educator and teacher rating scales) and formal (using assessment tools such as questionnaires and standardized testing). Both methods are effective and can help inform educators and parents about a child's progress.

Observation: The teacher observes the student at work or play in a natural environment. This can be done with minimal or no intrusion into children's activities. Or the teacher may be a participant in an activity. During this time, the teacher is noting how the child performed during the activity. The teacher observes the student's behavior and then records the data.

Teachers can also observe the child's emotional development (interaction with peers), linguistic ability (speaking and language development), social–emotional development (problem solving or interaction during social or free time), and physical development (during play and exploration time).

Portfolios: Portfolios are very useful as formative and summative assessments. They may be process or performance. The process portfolio is similar to a formative assessment, as the teacher collects data throughout the work phase or over a period of time. The process portfolio clearly shows the progress the child has made. The critical factor is the *feedback* the teacher provides to the student toward his improvement.

Performance portfolios can be used as a summative assessment, such as a rough draft before a final project. In the classrooms of the Reggio Emilia schools, documentation of children's learning is conducted by focusing intensively on their experience, memories, thoughts, and ideas as they work. Maintaining samples of a child's work at several stages of completion allows students, teachers, and parents to see how the child has progressed.

Portfolios are valuable to assess learning, as they contain comments written by the practitioners working with the children: transcriptions of children's discussions, comments, and explanations about the activity and comments made by parents. Observations, transcriptions of recordings, and photographs of children (with written parental/guardian permission) are also included, providing a wealth of information for the student and for a reader. Examples of the children's work and written reflections on the processes, in which the children are engaged, should be displayed in the classrooms and corridors. They will also serve as examples for a reflective process for other students.

Educator ratings: These are used by the teacher to rate a student's ability against a standard. Usually, a rubric is used to assess the student's ability, as well as a scale for ranking the activity. Rating scales have criteria for success based on expected outcomes and are clearly defined and detailed. They use a number system to rate from high to low with 1 being not proficient and 5 proficient. The range of numbers should always increase or decrease. For example, if the last number is the highest achievement in one section, the last number should be the highest achievement in the other sections.

Parent ratings: Parent ratings may be used to provide a broader picture of the student's ability because the student may act differently at home than in school. Parental input can be helpful to gather a complete picture of the student. Parents should be provided with rubrics for assessing their children. A multiple intelligences rating scale may be submitted to teachers, parents, and students, with the results being triangulated. This process provides an in-depth and comprehensive picture of the student. All stakeholders feel valued when using this tool.

Standardized tests: These are created to fit a set of testing standards. They are administered and scored and provide information for a summative evaluation. The value of a summative evaluation is that it provides data to determine if their curriculum is aligned to the test. Most teachers and administrators are reluctant to wait until the summative assessment, so they perform formative assessments to ensure that, during the summative assessment, the student will be successful.

Rubrics: In the preschool or kindergarten classroom, rubrics may be used to assess social, emotional, and cognitive domains of learning (figure 6.1). Sensory motor development, language development, and writing skills are also areas that lend themselves to a well-designed rubric. Designing a rubric is important, as one should keep in mind the objective or goal that the teacher or student has developed and then scaffold the learning in levels. None of the language in a rubric is negative, as it is a healthy self-challenge for the child toward self-regulation, self-dependent learning, and ultimately success. The teacher should always include the frequency of the action, the quality of the performance, and the application to situations. A teacher may post the rubric on the classroom wall, so that implementation and explanations are clear and concise and children understand what is expected of them.

The teacher can use a rubric developed for a specific project or a general rubric (scoring rubric) (table 6.1). Some or all facets of the project can be assessed. Distribute them to the students when they are working on an independent worksheet so they can modulate or regulate their learning. The teacher can use the rubric data for parent–teacher conferences and to show student progress.

Figure 6.1. Rubric Picture Data

Rubric for Kindergarten

Name: _____

Directions: Write a short story with 2-4 sentences.

Color in the bubble if you did it.

Draw a picture to go with your story.

	o USE CAPITALS
	o Use finger space 👆 between words.
	o End with a period ●
	o Reread your 👁👁 sentences.

Table 6.1. Chart Form of a Rubric for 1st–4th Grades

Giving a Speech	Emerging Proficiency (1)	Proficient (2)	Beyond Proficient (3)
Voice tone			
Speaking clearly			
Speech organized			
Introduction			
Body			
Conclusion			
Eye contact			
Score: 18–21 Beyond proficient 8–17 Proficient 1–7 Below proficient			

APPLYING ASSESSMENTS AND RUBRICS IN THE CLASSROOM THROUGH LESSON DESIGN

As you read through this lesson, you will find suggestions for application and correct timing of the use of assessments and rubrics in this example lesson. It will be clear to you that, as you teach a lesson, there is so much opportunity to get to know the nature of your learner and, through the use of rubrics, you will be creating a self-regulated learner, as well as a self-regulated, reflective classroom.

LESSON PLAN ON OUTER SPACE

Length of Lesson: Themed Project Approach lessons may last a week to a month (or longer) depending upon interest levels of students.

Note: In prekindergarten and kindergarten, the center areas are open daily. Free play is scheduled, a question of the day is posted, and the teacher conducts a large-group meeting and a small-group instruction. The teacher facilitates the lessons, and the assistant conducts reading aloud and art and assists when necessary, just to name a few of the daily activities. The day begins and ends with a reflection of the day and mindfulness moments. In 1st through 3rd grades, the teacher will designate an area of the classroom for free play and outer space exploration. There is a higher-leveled outer space center, data-collection worksheets, a teacher's lesson conducted with whole-group reflection time, and mindful moments, as well as the regularly scheduled day.

Title of Lesson: Outer Space

Student Learning Target (Objective): I will learn as much as I can about outer space and how it is different from our Earth.

Demonstration of Student Learning (DSL): I will be able to list all that I learned during free play about outer space. I will collect data about what I learned.

Essential Question: How is outer space different from the Earth on which we live?

Skills Addressed: Critical thinking, reading, writing, dramatic play, collaboration, investigation, data collection, observation, researching on the computer

Standards: Science 5.9 Astronomy and Space Science

A. Earth, Moon, Sun System
B. Solar System
C. Stars
D. Galaxies and Universe
(https://www.state.nj.us/education/cccs/2004/s5_science.pdf)

Readiness Set: The teacher will pose the thought of the day through a KWLH chart (assessment of leveled knowledge): what I *know* about outer space compared to our planet Earth and what I *want to learn* about outer space. This can be done as a whole group or in two groups prior to the lesson delivery. Next, read the book, *There's No Place Like Space: All About Our Solar System*, by Dr. Seuss.

Prior Knowledge: Some children know they live on Earth. They can recognize the globe in the classroom. They know the town and state in which they live. They know that the sky is above them and land and water are part of the Earth. They can refer to outer space as the galaxy, solar system, moon, stars, or planets. Some will discuss clouds, and others know about rockets, NASA, astronauts, space shuttles, amusement park exhibits, or movies and books about outer space. All children are adept at using data-collection sheets, as well as the computer for researching information.

Materials: Centers will include large cardboard refrigerator box (no assumption, but most likely this will become a space ship); cardboard boxes and paper towel tubes; aluminum foil and aluminum foil balls; space clothes, such as large boots, oversized work gloves, work helmets, and goggles; string or dryer duct tubing; paint in silver and gold, as well as other colors; compact disc of space-type music; data-collection sheets at center for writing (prekindergarten and kindergarten will use data-collection sheets to draw what they know about Earth and what they know about outer space; 1st, 2nd, and 3rd grades will use data-collection worksheets to compare and contrast Earth to outer space); computer; internet

Procedure: (Note: The procedure is up to the discretion of the teacher and staff. It will be happening simultaneously in all grades during free play, center work times, and throughout the day.)

1. Teacher sets up the rooms with space information, such as books in the library, music in the listening center, large cardboard box, paints, foil, and space-type materials, as well as space-type clothes, center with data-collection worksheets, and computer with internet access. An *observation assessment* can be made with minimal or no intrusion into children's activities. Educators can observe all facets of development, including intellectual, linguistic, social–emotional, and physical development, on a regular basis. The teacher may observe students as they go to the various centers and ask students open-ended questions. The teacher will ask probing questions (e.g., What is your plan for your project? What will you do if you have a problem? How will you know whether you are successful?) Overall, the observation assessment is based on what the teacher observes. The probing questions can lead to stretch or challenge questions.
2. The teacher will introduce space books, YouTube videos, and flannel board stories during story and whole-group times. The teacher will review learned knowledge and prior knowledge daily at reflection times. Children will extend learning by playing and exploring the subject and materials.
3. The teacher will provide the student with a rubric regarding the use of material (table 6.2).

An *educator rating scale* will be used for these types of tasks. The teacher will establish parameters for the students. For example, the student is directed to use a given number of books, gather information from the internet, or create a spaceship. When setting expectation levels, the rubric, or educator rating scale, would look like this: 1 book is rated as adequate, 2 books are partially proficient, 3 books are proficient, and 4 books would be exceeding expectations. Or the teacher may ask the students to watch a video from NASA. At the conclusion, the students would rate the video as adequate, developing, or proficient, and then explain to the teacher why they chose their rating.

Table 6.2. Materials Rubric

	Beginning	Progressing	Developed
Books	I used 1 book.	I used 2 books.	I used 3 or more books.
Internet	I looked at 1 site.	I looked at 2 sites.	I looked at 3 or more sites.
Student reflection	I prefer to use books because	I prefer to use the internet because	Next time, I will

Teacher notes: _____

4. Teacher will schedule free play and exploration of space materials for 45 to 60 minutes per day in prekindergarten and kindergarten classrooms and 30 minutes (or more if possible) in 1st-, 2nd-, and 3rd-grade classrooms. During this time, social and emotional skills may be observed and an educator rating scale may be used to determine what action plan needs to be developed, depending upon the age of the student. Here is an example of a rating scale for use in this lesson on social and emotional development (table 6.3). The teacher understands that this gives a general idea of what and when but is not written in stone, as we all develop at different rates.

Table 6.3. Social–Emotional Developmental Milestones

	Not Observed	*Emerging*	*Consistent*
Age 3			
Imitation and imagination emerging	—	—	—
Shows affection toward peers without prompting	—	—	—
Takes turns	—	—	—
Shows concern for a sad friend	—	—	—
Cares for dressing	—	—	—
Understands the idea of pronouns mine, yours, ours	—	—	—
Displays a variety of emotions	—	—	—
Separates family members	—	—	—
Age 4			
Enjoys new things	—	—	—
Likes to pretend	—	—	—
Plays with peers more	—	—	—
Cooperates	—	—	—

(continued)

Table 6.3. (*continued*)

	Not Observed	Emerging	Consistent
Role-plays familiar people	—	—	—
Discriminates fantasy and reality	—	—	—
Communicates feelings	—	—	—
Self-regulates	—	—	—
Age 5			
Wants to please the adult	—	—	—
Emulates friends	—	—	—
Enjoys rules	—	—	—
Enjoys dramatic play and movement	—	—	—
Self-aware	—	—	—
Developing independence	—	—	—
Developing cooperative skills	—	—	—
Less prompting needed	—	—	—
Strong social communication skills	—	—	—

(lesson plan cont.)

During whole-group times, the teacher will lead a discussion regarding our Earth and outer space, based on information the students are discovering. Discussions of creations, as well as imagery trips, would enhance the daily review. Students will draw things associated with outer space.

Portfolio assessment: At this point in the lesson, you will be assessing the students' progress over time, so you can see how the student has developed toward the goal or objective.

The key to the student's success is the feedback that you have been providing. If you have been clear and concise in your teaching, then by now the student knows what to do and how to correct mistakes. You will want to use rubrics in conjunction with portfolios, as it is shown to be highly effective for students to self-regulate their learning because the feedback helps them change the action plan and the rubric helps determine how to be successful.

The worksheets (homemade ones by the student, also called data-collection sheets, are part of portfolio assessment collections) that you have used throughout this lesson should be discussed in small-group times, so that children understand what is expected when completing a worksheet. Upon completion, the student will drop the worksheet into the "teacher's box." (Note: Students are given time to complete the worksheet, so there is no pressure on the student, which may inhibit exploration and playtime.)

Worksheets should be used to "grow" dendrites in that they serve a purpose tied to the assignment and challenge the learner. If the worksheet is *just busy work*, it has no value to the brain and learning process. When developing teacher-made worksheets, include verbs from the higher level of Revised Bloom Taxonomy (RBT), so that they promote metacognition.

You may decide to use a *standardized test* to find out what the children are learning. It may be a formative test to find out what has been learned or, if you are nearing the end of your lesson, you may use a summative test. These tests are administered and scored in a standard manner and are often used to assess the performance of children.

5. *Teacher questioning:* Teacher and staff circulate and prompt children who are not engaged and use appropriate questioning (open-ended) techniques to focus other children. For example, "I see that you are thinking about moving into the space area. I see that you have a long silver tube. Would you tell me how you think that can help in space? What do you think the wheel is for inside this box? Why is there so much silver? What are you called when you explore outer space? What do you eat in space? Where is the bathroom? What is gravity? And so on and so forth. (Reminder: This lesson is open to change, developmentally appropriate practice, differentiated instruction, and time management. This section is another opportunity for *observation assessment*.)

6. *Computer and internet* work regarding space: Students will look at pictures of space and pictures of Earth, so they can use this information for their data-collection charts (potential for portfolio assessment). A good use of the computer is from NASA's own site: https://www.nasa.gov/kidsclub/index.html.

Conclusion: Reconvene to finish the KWLH chart (figure 6.2). *What did you learn* and *how* did you learn it? Review and discuss what the group learned, as well as what they liked or disliked. Your KWLH chart is also a form of assessment, as it will give you ongoing process results and what you learned and how you learned it can be compared to the summative assessment.

Figure 6.2. Art Rubric

Rubric for Academics/1st through 5th grade

I am ready to work rating.	Not yet	Progressing	Got it	Reflection
I have my work in one place.	I have to gather my work.	I have some work ready.	All my work is assembled. I am ready.	What do I need to do to be prepared?
I will focus on the task.	I am not ready to learn.	I am not yet 100% focused.	I am focused and I know what I have to do.	How can I organize my desk or cubby space?
I am ready to begin the assignment.	I am not sure what to do.	I can begin the assignment but I still have some questions.	I know what to do and if I am stuck, I will ask two friends.	How can I self regulate my learning?
During the assignment	If I am stuck I will ask the teacher.	I will ask a friend what to do.	I will ask a friend or use resources in the room.	What will I do if I need help?
After the assignment	Next time I will...		I did and will continue to do....	What will I do differently? What will I do the same?
Reflection	I was organized and able to start the assignment.	I need to be better organized and focused during the lesson.	I was organized, focused and pleased with my performance.	Next time, I will ...

Assessment: As noted throughout this lesson, there are various assessments that can be written in the assessment section of the lesson.

Teacher self-evaluation or -reflection about lesson and changes to the lesson may conclude this lesson and be required in some school districts.

SUMMARY

This chapter has discussed rubrics and assessments and how each is used in the early childhood setting. Each was reviewed, and the reader should be prepared to make an intelligent decision about whether to use rubrics, assessments, or a combination of both in the early childhood learning environment. Rubrics are an essential part of lesson design, and examples of assessments and rubrics were explained in this chapter.

During the body of the lesson, assessment types were noted where they were most appropriate, and then its practical application during a lesson was presented for the reader. Self-regulation and self-dependent learning are the by-products of using rubrics, as rubrics level the development of the goal for the child. Samples of rubrics and assessments were suggested for kindergarten through 5th-grade classrooms, but with some minor adjustments in content, they can also be used in prekindergarten and upper grades.

Chapter Seven

Technology and the Early Childhood Learning Brain

FOCUS OF THE CHAPTER

In this chapter about technology and the early childhood learning brain, it is our intention to describe the nature of the learner. As you already know from reading this book, the nature of the learner, or how the learner learns, is instrumental in providing information to the teacher, so that he can develop engaging activities when writing lessons. If you apply Dr. Barbiere's Learner's Brain Model to the utilization of technology, you will easily learn how to correlate your classroom lessons with each of the stages of the Learner's Brain Model in mind.

FOCUS QUESTIONS FOR THE CHAPTER

1. Why am I using technology for lesson delivery?
2. How can I apply the Learner's Brain Model to technology utilization?
3. How can I apply this model to my classroom lessons?
4. How does a child's brain react when using technology?
5. How can I use technology to monitor students' progress, so they can become independent learners?

BACKGROUND

An enormous part of who we are is shaped by our experiences—experiences that today are defined by the pervasive influence of technology. This fact is particularly relevant in the case of children, both because children are the forefront of the technological revolution and because the developing brain is more malleable in response to experience than is the adult brain. The central question is not whether technology is affecting cognitive development—that is a given. The question is instead, how is technology affecting cognitive development? (D. Bavelier, C. S. Green, and M. W. G. Dye, "Children Wired—for Better and for Worse," *Neuron* 67, no. 5 (2010): 692–701).

As teachers you will establish the learning environment, so that technology enhances learning and student metacognition. The following is an example of an elementary school that is using technology for cognitive development.

A SAMPLE LESSON

It is Monday morning at 8:30 a.m., and you have just entered a kindergarten classroom. The sun is shining, and it's a lovely fall morning. There are 24 students in Mrs. X's classroom, and they are seated at tables, in groups of six per table. The teacher signals for the groups to take out their iPad tablets as she turns on the smart board (front of the room), from which she will project exactly what she wants the students to do on their personal computers.

The room is silent, and the teacher is providing direct instruction to her class. She begins with a Readiness Set by asking the students whether they can recall a fairy tale. This activates the students' prior knowledge and piques their interest. The purpose is to hook and connect the students' interest and prior knowledge with the new learning, thereby helping to bridge the gap of prior knowledge and new knowledge (the lesson). Next, she tells the class the name of the fairy tale they will be discussing today. After she tells the class the name of the fairy tale, she writes the title on the whiteboard so that she can begin using a multisensory approach in the instructional delivery.

After the Readiness Set, she lists the new and easy vocabulary words on her main screen, and the children type the same into their iPad word bank. As the lesson progresses, Mrs. X is now listing and drawing topics on the screen for each group to investigate: Group 1 is assigned characterization, group 2 plots, group 3 develops questions, and so on. The students begin silently working. There is no communication between groups at this point, and the only sound heard is the typing of students' fingers inputting information.

Mrs. X announces that tomorrow, during group time, the groups will share information with other members in their groups, and then on the third day, the entire class will share with each other.

Mrs. X is feeling very good about her technology lesson. She has the children cognitively engaged, as there are challenge words/tasks for each group based on their skill level, as well as tier 2 words. As the students work in their groups, she monitors the groups to collect data. She knows that engagement is different from compliance; engagement addresses the cognitive level of students (she knows that sitting in your seat is not engagement). She knows that, within her school department, she will be evaluated for her use of technology in the classroom, and she is hoping to receive high scores.

Mrs. X has used her own knowledge of "educational technology" to the best of her ability.

REFLECTION

What do you think about this lesson? Fill in table 7.1 based on the information that has been provided in this lesson thus far. Next, continue to read to see how you can add to or change your answers to further develop the lesson.

Table 7.1. Reflection Chart

	I think . . .	I would change . . .
Reflection		
Differentiated instruction		
Lesson delivery		
Cognitive development		
Communication		
Student collaboration		
Student engagement		
Notes		

TECHNOLOGY FULFILLS ADMINISTRATIVE REQUIREMENTS, BUT DOES IT SERVE A BETTER PURPOSE?

In this scenario, it is clear that the use of technology was to meet a requirement of the teacher, for the teacher. It was apparent in the last line of the vignette that this teacher was happy to use the technology to gain a score that would satisfy her teaching requirement. There are valuable attributes within this lesson, and, with some refinement, the teacher can gain better cognitive results from her students.

This lesson is not necessarily developmentally appropriate, as it was not as interactive as it could have been and was lacking differentiated instruction, guided instruction, practice, communication, and collaboration at the onset.

During this lesson, the smart board was used as an educational teaching tool with the children focused on the assignment. The teacher used picture clues, as well as easy vocabulary words. Noting that the class was silent signaled that all children were able to use the iPad by themselves and they were enjoying it. They were able to focus and follow the sequence of directions. In addition, there will be communication and information sharing during the upcoming days.

LESSON REFLECTION

When reflecting on the uses of technology in the classroom, it is described as an educational tool, but it can be used for entertainment as well. Furthermore, during any one lesson, it may be used both ways, as was apparent in Mrs. X's lesson. Mrs. X was using the smart board and the iPad as educational tools, and the students found the use of their tablet fun and entertaining.

As a teacher, you will want the lesson to be successful, as well as understand its value and learning benefits for your students. It should also serve as an assessment tool for you. To change this lesson so that it becomes more interactive, differentiated, collaborative, and communicative, follow these guidelines:

1. Interweave utilization of the smart board with the textbook. The smart board can access information to supplement the text. Using the smart board or iPad is useful to move from a visual, tactile experience to an interactive experience. The iPad or smart board can also include an interactive activity.

2. The smart board can access a variety of material from various sources. It may be useful in providing unfamiliar information to a student, so that the student can use the iPad or smart board to access the data.
3. Become familiar with the smart board and iPad to avoid problems during use.
4. Most importantly, have the students become familiar with the iPad so they can use the iPad on their own to regulate their learning.

When you are faced with the requirement of using a smart board in the classroom, try these suggested strategies:

1. Make sure you have learned the basics of its use. For example, learn how to turn it on. Many people do not know how to do this without prior instruction.
2. Take required or voluntary workshops, so that you can use the multitude of techniques supplied within the program.
3. Make sure all students can see the screen and that their tablets are hooked up to the main screen.
4. The children should be adept at being able to use the main screen and the tablet during the same lesson. This requires practice lessons.
5. Make sure your students can "at least" one-finger type.
6. Make use of colors and pictures for visual learners.
7. Make your lesson interactive, so that there is movement within the classroom. Students should be invited to the main screen and touch it for tactile input.
8. Save your students' work, so that they can review it from their home computer.
9. If you have a printer, be sure to print a hard copy for your students.
10. Use audio and visual signals for auditory learners.
11. Use the web, but make sure you have questionable sites blocked and that you have permission from administration to use the internet (The Teachers Guide website: http://www.theteachersguide.com/).

SAMPLE LESSON PLAN

Here is an exemplary sample lesson about fairy tales using the smart board.

Title: Cinderella, the Fairy Tale
Grade: Kindergarten–2nd Grade
Time: 2- to 3-Day Lesson

Student Learning Target (Objective): I will be able to define and explain the common characteristics of fairy tales (Stage 1 of the Learner's Brain Model: The Planning Stage).

Demonstration of Student Learning (DSL): I will be able to compare and contrast Cinderella and another book explaining the characteristics of Cinderella (Stage 1 of the Learner's Brain Model: The Planning Stage).

Essential Question: What makes a fairy tale different from a story? (Stage 1: The Planning Stage)?

Skills Addressed: Critical Thinking, Reading, Writing, Dramatic Play, Collaboration

Standards: Stage 1 of the Learner's Brain Model: The Planning Stage

- CCSS.ELA-Literacy.RL.3.1

Ask and answer questions to demonstrate understanding of a text, referring explicitly to the text as the basis for the answers.

- CCSS.ELA-Literacy.RL.3.2

Recount stories, including fables, folktales, and myths from diverse cultures; determine the central message, lesson, or moral and explain how it is conveyed through key details in the text.

- CCSS.ELA-Literacy.RL.3.3

Describe characters in a story (e.g., their traits, motivations, feelings), and explain how their actions contribute to the sequence of events.

- CCSS.ELA-Literacy.SL.3.1

Effectively engage in a range of collaborative discussions (one-on-one, in groups and teacher-led) with diverse partners on grade K–2 topics and texts, building on others ideas and expressing their own clearly.

Readiness Set: Stage 1 of the Learner's Brain Model: The Planning Stage

Ask the class how many have seen a Disney movie, such as *Cinderella*, *Pinocchio*, *Bambi*, *Dumbo*, or *Snow White*? Anyone who has not seen a Disney movie will be asked "What are some of the movies you have you seen lately?" (Hopefully, someone will have seen a fairy tale, and someone else will have seen a movie that is not a fairy tale.)

Procedure for Readiness Set: Stage 2 of the Learner's Brain Model: The Planning Stage

Secure a box of dress-up prince and princess clothes, including paper crowns, gloves, shoes, oversized dresses, hairnets for the wicked stepsisters, jackets, beads, and scarves. Children may choose to dress in clothes to experience the feeling of creativity and imagination.

Discuss how you feel "all dressed up." Discuss how you think the wicked stepsisters, the fairy godmother, the prince, and the princess feel. Use open-ended questioning to solicit feeling responses.

Instructional Delivery: Whole-Group Instruction (Stage 3 of the Learner's Brain Model: Instructional Delivery for Large-Group Discussion)

Ask the students "What is a fairy tale?" As they answer the question, ask a scribe to write or draw pictures with the answers on a piece of chart paper at the front of the room (most often the kindergarten child will name fairy tales like Little Red Riding Hood. This is acceptable, and the scribe should draw a girl in a red cape, etc.).

The teacher writes the answer/definition on the smart board: *A fairy tale is a children's story about magical and imaginary beings and lands. It is a story that is made up (or fabricated) and uses a bit of trickery or deception as a theme. It is a fantasy story that usually ends up happy, but can be scary at times* (when teaching early grades, be sure to use developmentally leveled language).

Teacher Reaffirms the Student Learning Target:

Today, you will be demonstrating how you use your sequencing skills by adding one sentence at a time, on the main board, to create a new fairy tale.

Instructional Delivery Activities: Stage 3 of the Learner's Brain Model: Instructional Delivery

On chart paper, compare and contrast the students' answers with the teacher's definition on the smart board. Then, name similarities and differences in the two types of stories.

Direct Instruction: Stage 3 of the Learner's Brain Model: Instructional Delivery

Ask the students to gather around and begin to read aloud Cinderella. Choose a version that is not too long. Say "What makes Cinderella a fairy tale?" (See definition above; compare and contrast.)

Once the story is read and you have checked for understanding, begin a discussion of common themes within the story. These themes will correlate with the definition (e.g., magical, princesses and princes, wicked sister, fairy godmother, fantasy, use of words such as "Once upon a time," etc. See list of characteristics of a fairy tale).

- Assign roles to the students, and allow them to act out the parts of Cinderella in sequence. Use main idea, character traits, themes, and the language to guide you into small, sequential vignettes of Cinderella.
- Invite the children to write their own fairy tale by using the smart board. Tell the students that you will begin the fairy tale by writing a few sentences on the smart board. Next, give each child a turn to use his finger (or older children, the smart board writing tool) to add to the story. This is a rebus story. Pictures will be included.
- Teacher writes "Once upon a time, there was a castle in a great land called _____ (teacher will draw a castle in a fancy land). There were many children in this land, and they were in charge of everything (teacher will draw many diverse characteristics of boys and girls). They were all happy, until one day, a wicked witch came to their town (teacher will ask a student to come up and draw a wicked witch) and so on.
- Each child will take a turn writing a sentence or drawing a picture (with guidance) to add to the sentence before his own. Help can be given by peers and the teacher if necessary to keep the story on track.

Consolidation for Closure: Stage 4 of the Learner's Brain Model: Consolidation for Closure

Ask the students what they learned today. Discuss main idea, characterization, setting, details, and other parts of a fairy tale.

Active Monitoring and Assessment: Stage 4 of the Learner's Brain Model: Consolidation for Closure

The teacher will use Active Monitoring as a form of assessment. It will be ongoing and informal during the play. Reading can be assessed formally, as well as the writing assignment. Encourage participation and support, and facilitate the children throughout the lesson.

The teacher may assign another fairy tale, including the common themes and the moral of the story. Fairy tales have morals and can be used as continuing education throughout the school year.

Assessment Note: Stage 4 of the Learner's Brain Model: Consolidation for Closure

The teacher will assess each student's ability in the following areas:

1. Ability to apply the definition of a fairy tale when writing their sentence or drawing their picture.
2. Ability to show motivation and actions to complete the story.
3. Ability to sequence in an orderly fashion.
4. Ability to complete thoughts when writing a fairy tale collaboratively (figure 7.1).

Figure 7.1.   Art Rubric

Rubric for Kindergarten

Student Name: _____

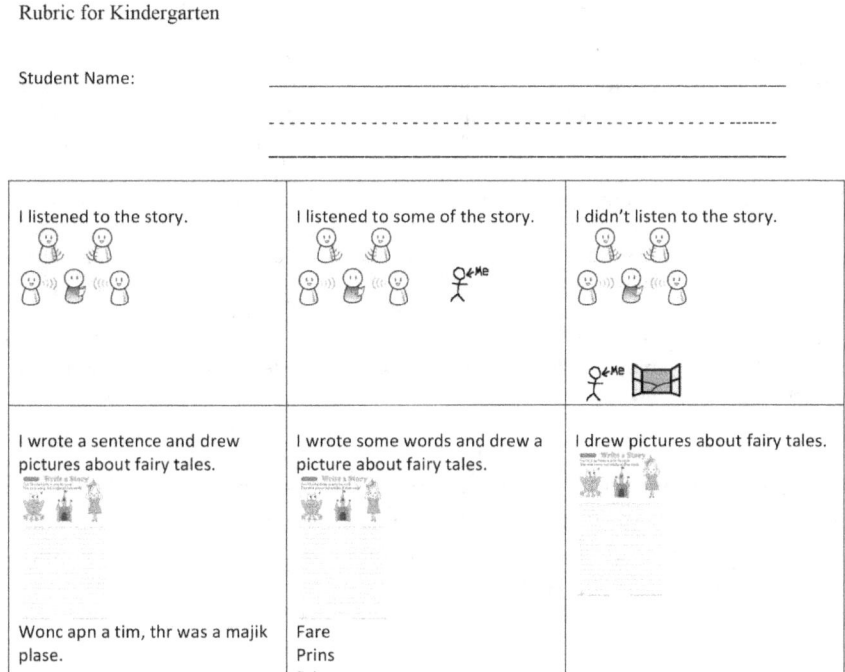

In addition, the teacher will assess the understanding of the literature though dramatic play in order to clarify common themes and morals of a fairy tale. Use the rubric in table 7.2 to score each student.

Table 7.2. Chart Rubric for Fairy Tales Grades 1 and 2

Name	4	3	2	1
Reading	Understands all of what is read	Understands most of what is read	Understands some of what is read	Understands little of what is read
Sequencing	Excellent display of story sequencing/ 6 events in order	Good display of story sequencing/ 4 events in order	Fair display of story sequencing/ 3 events in order	Poor display of story sequencing/ 2 events in order
Understanding character	Text and pictures describe character fully	Text and pictures describe character partially	Text and pictures describe character slightly	Text and pictures do not match character
Understanding setting	Text and pictures describe setting fully	Text and pictures describe setting partially	Text and pictures describe setting slightly	Text and pictures do not match setting
Illustrations and text in technology	Illustrations match and add to text	Illustrations match text	Illustrations attempt to match text somewhat	Illustrations do not match text

When writing a fairy tale, include all of the elements in table 7.3 in your story, checking them off as you proceed. (Make this directive developmentally appropriate, as kindergarten may do one or two and older grade children should use many characteristics.)

Table 7.3. **Checklist for Common Elements of Fairy Tales**

	Element	Y/N	Comment
1	"Once upon a time" to begin your story		
2	Princesses, princes, kings, queens, and royalty		
3	Humans can be different, such as giants and dwarfs		
4	Animals are often animated and have certain powers or abilities		
5	Setting is often enchanted, including kingdoms, castles, and forests		
6	Magic is used by characters good and bad		
7	Innocent, good characters, subjected to evil or something wrong		
8	The antagonist is in conflict with a main character in the story		
9	Problems and solutions for the protagonist or hero		
10	"They lived happily ever after" ending		
11	Fairy tales can often teach a lesson/moral		

Reflection

Source: https://www.rcsdk12.org/cms/lib04/NY01001156/Centricity/Domain/5350/CHECKLIST%20FOR%20FAIRY%20TALES.pdf.

As the reader, take time to reflect and compare Mrs. X's initial lesson to the improved lesson. Why is the delivery of this lesson more developmentally appropriate than Mrs. X's lesson? What is the cognitive value of this lesson as compared to Mrs. X's lesson?

MERGING TECHNOLOGY INTO A LESSON

It is apparent that merging Mrs. X's lesson, which was technology based, with that of a hands-on lesson would be beneficial. The use of technology in the classroom is a learning experience for students. It is included in many evaluation instruments and mandatory during the lesson. By incorporating technology, with the lesson-based theme on fairy tales, one will find the creative process augmented.

In this book, the milestones of childhood development have been reviewed, and now you should have a better understanding of why marrying technology with hands-on experiences is essential. In addition, you will be able to make your own comparisons to Mrs. X's lesson versus the fairy-tale lesson.

Collaboration, creativity, creative thinking, and communication are apparent in both lessons but much stronger in the second version of the lesson, which includes all of the above *and* a technology piece. In addition, curiosity is what makes the child interested in learning. By expanding this lesson to use technology in cross-curricular ways, it will intrigue the learner and help to scaffold learning.

INCORPORATION IS THE KEY

Incorporation of technology is the answer to having an integrated lesson balanced between teacher instruction and technology. It is also important to the incorporation of the disciplines. Integration of science through the use of digital microscopes and video conferencing for math, language arts, and social studies fits perfectly in this lesson design.

Encourage reading about castles, and look for countries that have castles, kings, and queens to extend the learning through technology. Other forms of technology include Skyping and FaceTime, which can be fun and educational. Actually, FaceTiming with a real duchess of England and finding out how she became a duchess would lend itself to this fairy-tale lesson. The use of technology enhances the lesson in a meaningful way and is an excellent use of technology.

Teachers can use technology to capture pictures of the children at work and play and then display them around the room. This is a good example of using technology in an interactive way. It is important that the teacher follows school and district policies and procedures regarding student photos.

Digital storytelling can be added to this lesson as another way of using technology in a positive way. Storing the stories on the computer and instructing the child to retrieve and add to her file is an important way for the child to become a self-dependent learner, as well as a creative one. Special needs children with physical and emotional disabilities will need adaptive applications to remove challenging barriers to learning. A child's home language can be added to the technology for a complete linguistic experience.

A common form of technology that has a preconceived notion as negative is video gaming. Video gaming may be thought of as a teen addiction, but truth be told, video gaming is affecting children as young as five years of age.

The instant dose of dopamine, or the feel-good hormone, sends a signal to children's brains that this is wonderful and makes them feel great; they love getting rewarded. When you remove the game after this euphoric feeling, there is no dopamine, and the children lack the ability to understand what to do to feel good. During the readjustment period, the children may react with anger, stress, and mood swings and may even withdraw for a time. When students play video games, the blue and white light from the screen stimulates toddlers' brains. When children use the iPad before bed, the blue light will trick the brain into thinking that it is still daylight.

The Learner's Brain Model outlines the five stages of gaming. Gamers of all ages select safe, nonthreatening environments that are primed to learn the task. A classroom emulates this for the students by establishing rules, protocols, and clear consequences for appropriate actions.

In addition, the gamer sets goals from beginning level to a higher level, through various strategies and techniques. The student has a target objective, as well as an achievable goal. Through these goals, the gamer takes onus for object, idea, or person. The gamer uses feedback in the most essential way, to continue his quest to the goal. When the gamer has reached the most difficult level, he looks for insight into how to win the game. Finally, the last stage is reflection, whereas the gamer reviews in his mind what he did to become successful.

Video games are adaptive and provide immediate feedback to the gamer. Good choices are rewarded, and bad choices provide learning opportunities and the chance to try again, aiding with self-regulation, self-correction, and self-monitoring behaviors. Video games provide rewards or incentives in the form of bonus points and incremental successes. Gamers learn to use patterns to help them navigate through complex sets of inputs with hundreds of features and make decisions-based comparisons.

If we apply the Learner's Brain Model to the classroom, the scope and sequence is the same for the young child who is learning how to read. He uses technology with guided assistance from the teacher in the classroom while using *Leap Frog* until he masters the technology himself. He learns the features of the game, patterns, how to make decisions, how to choose correct answers, all while monitoring his own learning with bells and whistles from the "frog teacher."

The student can move to the next level, if he completes the objective correctly, or move back to repeat what was not learned, without any negative consequences. This for the learning brain is monumental. It is a true motivational tool.

The question remains as to how much is enough when using games like *Reader Rabbit* and *Leap Frog*? Nothing replaces a book in hand. The romance of having a book in your lap in the reading corner, all cozy, is a wonderful way to captivate the early reader into learning, although using video games in the early childhood classroom has a place as a learning tool, reinforcement for skills learned, and as a fun way to introduce simple concepts. The special needs population does very well with the repetitive nature and patterning and immediate feedback found in video games.

HOW CAN VIDEO GAME STRATEGIES BE APPLIED TO THE EARLY CHILDHOOD CLASSROOM?

Why can youngsters play video games for hours, but struggle to pay attention and focus on classroom tasks? Learners, in fact, can attend to and focus on classroom tasks when the material is challenging and has meaning. They also attend when they can make sense of what is being taught and see patterns and relationships of the parts to the whole.

TECHNOLOGY, THE BRAIN, AND THE EARLY CHILDHOOD YEARS

The first three years of life are the most significant period of a child's development, especially for the brain, which is growing faster than any other part of the body. During this developmental time, a child's brain benefits from stimulation and is more receptive to positive influences than negative ones. Apply this concept to the use of technology.

By the time the child reaches six years of age, her eye and hand coordination is refined and she is eager to use technology. Children can be taught at an early age how to use technology with their little fingers. As a teacher, one must remember that writing can be affected if technology is overused. Teachers have reported that handwriting skills are on a decline. Many school districts are now adding a handwriting curriculum to their classrooms because teachers are observing a lack of fine motor development. School-age children who could hold a crayon correctly or use scissors when they started school are now lacking those skills when entering in September. Children are doing less with their hands, and clay-dough and sensory art are a thing of the past in some households.

TEACHING GOOD TECHNOLOGY HABITS

Most recently, while eating at a restaurant at the Jersey Shore, a couple and their young son were sitting at a table. The parents were on their smartphones while the son was playing with his iPad, with little or no conversation taking place.

The food was delivered by the waitress. The parents put their phones away and readied themselves to eat while simultaneously beginning a conversation. No one directed the five-year-old child to put away his iPad as his food arrived. The parents were now happily eating their dinners and in full conversation mode, while the child's food remained untouched and getting cold. Do you know how fast fish turns cold and gelatin-like? YUCKO! A sure bet is that many of you have seen this occurrence in your daily lives, but have you stopped to think about the message we are sending the young learner?

As a new or seasoned teacher, can you imagine telling the parents at "Back to School Night" that in *your* class, *you* will be allowing the children unlimited time for iPad use for all of their schoolwork. Do you think parents would be happy to know that during the day their child has an iPad babysitter?

TO BE OR NOT TO BE

When technology first entered classrooms many years ago, all of it was battery operated. Tape recorders, phonographs, and compact disc players were considered new technology. Fast-forward 15 years, and we are faced with technology that is much more sophisticated. Teachers and support staff were forced to adapt for record keeping, professional development, and attendance. Many classroom teachers found this hard, and many did not succumb to the adaptation, retiring instead because they truly believed technology could not replace the teacher and student relationship in learning. The remaining teachers soon realized that the technology era was here to stay, and they learned to integrate the technology with supervision and common sense.

A master teacher quickly understands that technology can present issues regarding social interaction skills and that targeting this skill cannot be forgotten or replaced. In other words, if you had the choice of going to Disneyland or watching Disneyland on YouTube, which would you choose? The sensory experience of actually being present in Disneyland includes sounds, sights, smells, tastes, and touches that you would never experience on the YouTube video, no matter how magnificent the technology. Even the 3-D versions cannot compare to actually being there. The outside time that you are spending with your child, as well as the communication you are having, is so valuable.

An iPad cannot provide that human interaction. Yes, you can get a lot of chores done in the house while your child is on the iPad, but as a teacher, one knows that language exchanges and development, social skills and friendships, and the emotional freedom of being in a wonderful atmosphere are missing from technology.

FROM THE HOUSE TO THE CAR

Our vans and cars are equipped with television screens to keep the children entertained and quiet while we drive long (or even short) distances. We know that there is a benefit to cognitive development with educational programs, while others are purely entertainment or used for babysitting. The latter would do very little for good cognitive development, unless the child were an avid reader with strong comprehension skills.

Research suggests that school-age children (four to five years old) can benefit from educational videos and television if they are exposed to a maximum of one to two hours a day. For instance, *Dora the Explorer* and the *Sesame Street* television series have helped to increase language development, vocabulary, and expressive and receptive language, as well as math skills, in their viewers. Unfortunately, the same cannot be stated for all educational television shows, as some have shown a decrease in language and math learning. In addition, a rise in obesity due to lack of exercise from using technology inside the home and eyesight strain from too much screen time, hyperactivity, and shortened attention spans are all reported to date.

WELCOME TO MR. ROGER'S NEIGHBORHOOD

The iconic Fred Rogers of the acclaimed *Mr. Roger's Neighborhood* hosted 895 episodes of children's educational television between 1968 and 2001. He was an advocate for early education programming, which aligned itself with child psychologists and child development experts. Mr. Rogers was a pioneer in children's television, demanding that every episode be calculated to teach in the most positive manner possible, or the show would not be aired. In his approach to educational television, he was acutely determined to make it developmentally appropriate for his viewers. As technology became faster and steadfast in children's lives, Mr. Rogers remained committed to keeping it slow paced, thoughtful, and purposeful.

WHAT WOULD MARIA MONTESSORI SAY ABOUT THE IPAD?

Dr. Maria Montessori believed that children learn best when their environment supports their natural desire for learning. She believed that it is essential for children to learn through experiences that empower the mind, spirit, and body. Her approach to education was based on a self-directed methodology, as well as hands-on learning in a classroom where children were able to make guided creative choices in their own learning. The teacher or facilitator offered choices based on the children's interests and offered developmentally appropriate activities to guide the learning process.

Below is a simple Venn diagram to compare a version of Dr. Montessori's philosophy statement and the definition of technology as we know it today. As one would surmise, we find a strong overlap in the center of the Venn diagram as shown in figure 7.2.

Figure 7.2. Venn Diagram

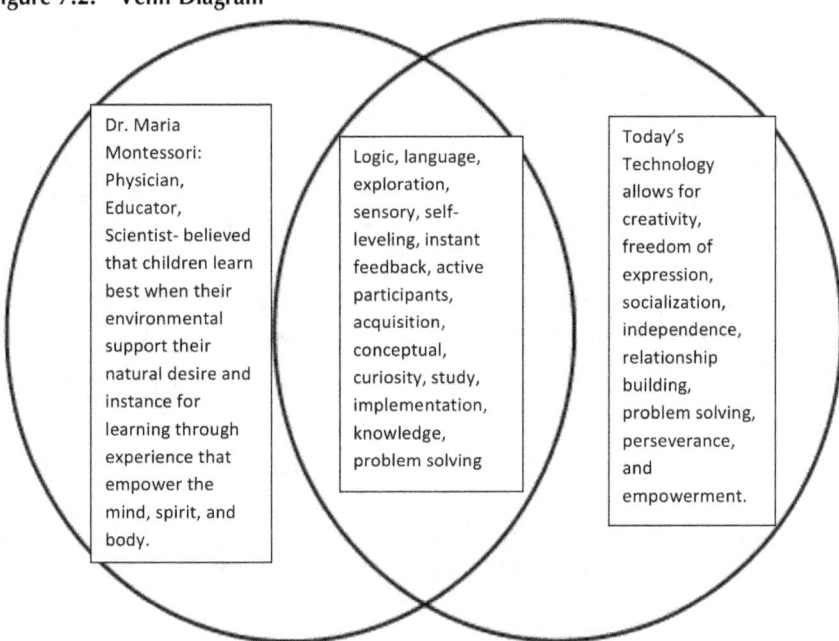

It is apparent that the way learning is delivered is the most important component for cognitive development. If we compare Fred Rogers's desire to deliver material that was diverse and developmentally appropriate through educational television programming; Maria Montessori's hands-on, interactive scaffold learning objectives; and the Learner's Brain Model, we have a model for scaffolding lessons based on meaningful experiences and brain research.

HOW CAN I USE TECHNOLOGY IN THE CLASSROOM?

The answer is to establish guidelines for teachers and parents that allow for the supervised use of technology. Time constraints, guidance while using technology, communication about the content, and selecting the most developmentally appropriate learning game for the nature of your learner would be a great place to begin.

Classroom teachers, as well parents, should encourage discussion after technology use, assist with regulation of the child's moods after gaming, and foster relationships with peers to build friendships and encourage social skills and communication. Find an "unplugged" time each day for self-reflection, and keep self-reflection at the forefront of the thought processes while encouraging the use of all five senses to build a strong cognitive development within your early childhood person.

HOW CAN I USE TECHNOLOGY TO PROMOTE THE GOALS FOR MY CURRICULUM WHILE MAINTAINING THE MENTAL AND PHYSICAL HEALTH OF MY STUDENTS?

Here is the National Association for the Education of Young Children's guidelines for teachers, which can be applied to parents as well, with some modifications.

GUIDELINES FOR USING TECHNOLOGY

1. Information about cultural, linguistic, and developmental appropriateness must guide the selection of technology and interactive media.

a. Integrate technology into early childhood programs and do not replace creative play, multisensory explorations, social interactions, or physical activities indoors and outdoors.
   b. Use a large selection of classroom materials, linguistic, cultural, and developmental.
   c. Be cognizant of developmental level, age appropriateness, background, and abilities of the child.
   d. Technology should not be used with children under two years of age.
2. Technology should be used to support the ways in which young children learn, maximize home-school connections, and assess children's progress.
   a. Use hands-on, engaging, and empowering technology and media. Give the child control. Provide adaptive scaffolds to ease the accomplishment of tasks and use technology to support children's learning.
3. Technology should be integrated into children's daily activities and used to enhance adaptations for dual language learners and children with special needs.
   a. Use during free-choice and small-group activities.
   b. Assistive technology can enable equitable access for children with special needs.
   c. Support the home language and enhance the English language for dual language learners.
4. Teachers, children, and families need guidance in becoming discerning users of technology.
   a. Educate teachers and families in the selection and proper use of technology.
   b. Children require guidance to operate technology properly and safely, setting limits and avoiding inappropriate content.
   c. Adults must be responsible for children and protect them from exploitation.

(Source: "Early Childhood Program Guidance for Children Ages Birth through Eight" found in its entirety on the NAEYC website.)

Make wise decisions, and please don't fall captive to the pressures of society. This chapter and the entire book is designed to give you insight into making the right decisions, so that your children will desire to learn through their own actions and reactions. Your early childhood students should learn to tap into their own intrinsic motivations and create building blocks of control, competence, problem solving, questioning, thinking, and critiquing.

SUMMARY

As discussed previously, the role of technology is to enhance a lesson and not provide busy work or an add-on to a lesson that is not integrated into the person or does not enhance the lesson. The guidelines of technology should be used to support the ways in which young children learn, maximize home-school connections, and assess children's progress. Additionally, technology should be integrated into children's daily activities and used to enhance adaptations for dual language learners and children with special needs.

To help incorporate the Learner's Brain Model into lesson design, a sample lesson was provided to showcase how each section of the lesson plan relates to brain research and the Learner's Brain Model.

How the child's brain reacts to technology is important, so it is necessary for teachers to plan lessons that infuse technology effectively and efficiently. Technology should be a resource that enhances the lesson and not just a mode for visual stimulation or an activity to pass time. Technology must be related to purpose, purpose, and purpose.

Chapter Eight

Tying It All Together

FOCUS OF THE CHAPTER

In the previous chapters, we addressed student empowerment, the nature of the learner, classroom environment, play and exploration, lesson design, rubrics and assessments, and technology. In this chapter, we will instruct you regarding the implementation of our strategies and techniques from the previous chapters and lead you into implementing them during the first few days of school. It is our intention to guide you through the beginning of a new school year and help you to develop and maintain an atmosphere conducive to learning while simultaneously setting into motion these practices.

You will begin on the first day of school by implementing our strategies and then continue to use the practical application of the skills throughout the school year. Once your colleagues witness you in action, they will support you and join in creating a strong foundation for a whole-school program. Parents will marvel at your skills and ability to regulate your students. You will find yourself becoming a natural at the techniques and strategies. You may even find yourself extending this approach to meet your home/school connection requirement.

FOCUS QUESTIONS FOR THE CHAPTER

1. How do I implement the theory and practice outlined in this book into my classroom?
2. Why do I want to implement a positive behavior program?

BACKGROUND

As a teacher, you will have many thoughts and plans in your mind before you enter the classroom. It seems from experience that this is just the nature of the teacher. You may be thinking about your support staff and their assignments, student seating arrangements, time management, organizational skills, planning lessons, and the diverse student body and their parents, and of course, you will be thinking about how you will begin implementing *The Student Empowerment Program* so that your commitment ensures that all stakeholders have a stress-free year. The positive behavior strategies, student self-regulation skills, and self-modulation of student learning are your target objectives from here on.

Throughout this book, you have read about techniques, strategies, and theories and learned about the early childhood brain. Now, it is time to bring all that information to the front of your mind and tie it together. You will begin by establishing a working environment conducive to learning that that is positive, calm, safe, and secure for the early childhood persons in your care.

The Student Empowerment Program can stand alone as a separate program or it may be incorporated with your school's policies. No matter which you choose, you will find that, when you implement *The Student Empowerment Program* and the 5Rs, they will become second nature to you and your teaching regimen.

BEFORE THE OPENING DAY OF SCHOOL

Some teachers are not required to "work" before school opens, so if this is your case, then please make sure you have these things in order on the first day to prevent unstructured chaos. You do not want to present unprepared to the children.

RESPONSIBILITY: THE FIRST *R*

1. Before the students enter the classroom is a critical time because you will want to learn everything you can about the students. You may have sent a letter to their homes during the summer, and you may have a multiple intelligence survey in your possession. It's time to read it and make mental and anecdotal notes. Once you begin understanding your students, you will be able to plan lessons based on what they are capable of doing and then set high expectations for them.
2. Please double-check with the school nurse to make sure you have not missed any pertinent information associated with the safety and care of your students. The nurse will supply you with information regarding medications or health modifications (*establishing a safe and secure environment*).

TYING IT ALL TOGETHER • 115

3. You will want to know who has permission to go home with whom, who is taking the bus, and other similar housekeeping items. Any guardianship or legal situations should also be noted by you in your personal notebook.

Knowing your students' needs will help them become responsible for such things as classroom management, when they go to the nurse for medication, taking the bus or preparing to walk home, and learning how to be responsible during work/learning centers and playtimes.

Setting up the Physical Environment and Atmosphere

4. At some point, you have set up the physical space (*classroom environment*) of the classroom, and it is ready for the children. This is important, as the care and navigation of the physical space will be taught to the students in the first few days. The room (which belongs to the teacher and the students) should be constructed as an "aid" to learning. By displaying rubrics, charts, posters, alphabet letters, numbers models, weather information, center information, etc., you will be empowering your students to learn.

OPENING DAY OF SCHOOL AND THE BEGINNING OF SELF-REGULATION

5. First impressions are lasting and go a long way toward respect, so greet the children with your sincere smile and treat them the way you wish to be treated. Children will always remember how you make them feel.
6. Once in the classroom, immediately begin to show the children how to use the closets and storage units for their items. If you have parents with you (some schools welcome parents and others do not), ask them to sit quietly and watch from a distance if possible. Some children will have trouble separating (*begin creating a secure and safe classroom environment*).

Forcing a child to separate is not suggested and you may have to discuss your feelings with your supervisor prior to the beginning of school or talk to the principal to determine what the school policy is on separation. Hopefully, your philosophy is open to parents but this may be different from the school's. A child who is crying is going to need extra support and adjustment time before allowing separation from his mom or dad. Be patient, supportive, cool, and calm, and reassure the child that his mom, dad, or guardian will be back to get him after school.

During this time, begin telling the child what you see him doing to aid in the regulation process. Continue *The Student Empowerment Program* by observing and building successes a little at a time. For example, for the crying child, say "I see you are breathing calmly and that you are looking around the room." Continue to observe your students, so you may plan accordingly (*creating a safe and secure environment, building rapport, breathing methods introduced, and beginning regulation*).

For the older child who is accustomed to school, state "You have been so wonderful at hanging up your jacket and keeping your books off the floor and your feet on the floor. You are showing me you know how to regulate your behavior." (*These strategies help to promote self-regulation, self-esteem, listening skills, and rules.*)

Open-Ended Questions and Observations

7. Begin a tour of the classroom. The first stop is the bathroom; whether it's in the room or the hallway, please be sure the students know where it is. It's time to locate it. After you locate it, discuss the rules, and show the bathroom passes to use when they must go to the lavatory (*building trust and responsibility*). The instruction is for each person to look to see whether there is a pass available and use it when it is necessary without asking "to be excused." This saves time from interruptions and allows for more teaching time. First, everyone will want to try it, but with little attention given to the task, it will fade into a normal routine.

Continue to show and explain all of the areas of the room, and ask *open-ended questions* regarding familiarity, likes, and dislikes. For example, "Who knows what goes on in this center? What do we do with that big white screen in the front of the room?" Scaffold your questions to help build understanding.

Continue to use *The Student Empowerment* phrases while the children are walking and observing. "I see this group can follow rules, and we haven't even discussed them yet. This is amazing, and I am so thrilled with your behavior. You are all so on target." You will be verbally rewarding the positive, so they become familiar with hearing positive comments and learn the expectations and rules before they have a chance to make mistakes and break them.

Reflection: The Second *R*

8. Gather the students together in a whole group, and begin a simple reflection exercise. Try this one to learn names.

Tell the children they have the opportunity to speak in this circle time while they are holding a fuzzy, soft, or squishy ball (*ball creates safe and secure feeling and aids in independent turn taking*). Direct them to say their name and give a word about themselves that begins with the *same letter as their name*, for instance, "Frank and funny." Most prekindergarten and kindergarten children will be able to state their name and then give you a word about themselves, such as "Frank and tall."

As you progress with this game during the week, you may ask the children to state their name, name another classmate in the group, and then give two examples, one being something about themselves and the other being something about the friend. Older children can maintain the alliteration theme, while younger children may randomly describe until they learn sounds.

Regulation: The Third *R*

9. Depending upon the grade you teach, your students will be directed with music signals to go to desks, tables, or centers. Prior to going to centers, you will want to introduce the preschool or kindergarten children to a few centers at a time and show them how to take a bracelet to limit how many people are in one center at a time. The bracelet will not be used when the children learn to regulate, as they will be able to regulate turn taking very soon. (*When the children observe and wait for entrance into a center, you are teaching self-regulation skills. Explain to the students you want them to be independent learners, and encourage taking part in their learning. Use developmentally appropriate language to make your point*).

The older early childhood students will understand that, when they hear the calm music played, it is time to go to their desk or table and take out their journal, workbook, textbook, and so on. (*instilling self-regulation based on a music cue*).

Continue to play the music during the work session. Classical music can upset some children, so you may want to use nature music or serene-type cultural music (*teaching diversity and tolerance for other cultures and respect of nature*).

10. During open-ended playtime (for prekindergarten and kindergarten), snack and milk can be incorporated into this block of time (*fostering independence, self-dependent learning, and self-regulation*). For the first few days, the assistant will help the children retrieve their snack and model how to share a provided snack (*after learning the task of self-serve, it becomes self-regulated action, as well as math, science, or nutrition skill building*). The assistant discusses the portion size with the children during the first few days and then trusts the children to accomplish eating the snack. The assistant socializes with them and helps only when necessary (*support staff building rapport*).
11. Throughout the school year, the adults are building relationships with the children and learning something about each one of them. Follow up with conversations to show the children you are interested in them (*communication skills, trust, safe and secure environment*).
12. Depending upon the grade, there will be transition times in and out of the day. After the first center/work time and snack for the younger children, you may want to gather the entire group for music and dance. The older children may be going to "specials" with other teachers in other rooms. This is the time for *transitions*, and you will want them to be smoothly executed. Encourage students to lead the way during transitions to begin fostering independence.
13. Transitions are often called the hardest part of the day. They can become rushed, chaotic, and stressed. It is highly suggested that you use your observation skills and cite what you wish the children to do before they do it. You can also use little games, songs, movement exercises, and addition and subtraction quizzes to move children from one area to another smoothly. The goal is to have a signal for transitions, so students know what to do when they hear the signal.

Remember to tell the children you see them standing just like the example you have posted on the wall for "walking in the hallway." You will want to tell them exactly what you want them to do, by stating that they are doing it before you even ask them to do it. Or you may say "I only had to ask once, and look at this group; you knew how to do this so well" (such as walking in the hallway, getting ready for work by having pencils sharpened before you begin your lesson, etc.). The same will hold true for returning to the classroom.

Positive Behavior Modification/Add-On

14. Upon returning, you may find the behavior modification reward chart is in order. This is an add-on, and you certainly do not have to use it.

A whole group of children may be rewarded with a special free time, healthy treat party, or free homework passes when they reach a goal on "Fun Friday."

15. At this time in the day, you may read a story to transition back to another academic lesson. The story will help reengage the students back to the classroom environment after being in a special for 30 minutes or more. The story may be prefaced by a reflection time of what they did before they came back to the classroom and a reflection of their own actions and behavior. Using thumbs-up or thumbs in the middle could help the children reflect upon whether they are happy with their own behavior or need improvement. Note, there are no thumbs-down in this exercise. Keep it positive (*reflection to regulation*).

This can also be a time for problem solving in your "camp of concern" group time (*by giving names to group times, activities, work times, etc., you are engaging the children to listen for the cue and become self-dependent. You will see that they will "run" over to the session and begin to develop a sense of ownership of the classroom*).

16. During the academic lesson, you will continually observe the students to build success even before you start the lesson. You may find you sound scripted, but that will change as you develop your repertoire of words and phrases that are meaningful and actually send messages to the children's brain that you are viewing them and approving and supporting their positive behavior, such as "I see that you did that the first time I asked." Something as simple as that tells the children they are important to you because they are good listeners (*review rule chart without actually using the rule chart builds reflection, rules, and regulation*).

17. You may have a beehive with the names of each child on Velcro so that, when you see them doing something that is positive during the lesson, you will move their bee one stripe up in the hive. All of the bees move up, and even the child who is struggling to conform and regulate gets his bee moved up for something that you build in the way of a success. Never move backward on the hive or any similar chart.

For instance, here's a scenario with two students, Martha and James. Without any words, just a knowingly positive nod, you will move Martha's bee to hive line 2. Martha smiles and makes eye contact with you (or maybe not). You can see her lift her head and shoulders and an air comes over her as she begins to concentrate or challenge herself more since you noticed her.

James is finding it difficult to concentrate and is looking out of the window frequently. You may walk over to James and whisper to him "James, you have your pencil out, your book is open to the correct page, and your eyes are focused on your work. James your bee is up a notch!" Hint: It is better to notice James before he begins daydreaming. Once he is daydreaming, he will not appreciate your observation as much. So, if you know that James is a daydreamer many days, you will want to capture his moment *before* he begins to drift. For instance, "James, your eyes are focused on your work, and your bee is moving up another notch!" You will not say "James, take your eyes off the window and focus on your work," as that would be negative and only embarrass the child. Older children prefer personal connections, and younger children like being positively noted in front of their peers.

Was James's eyes really focused, and was he really engaged when you built that success? The answer is no, but this observation will go a long way to help James regulate. So keep up this good work.

What is the difference between Martha and James? The difference is that you will soon not have to move Martha's bee up a notch because Martha is internalizing her behavior as positive and will no longer be needing an external reward. Of course, you will continue to tell Martha how well she is doing and commend her for her successes and accomplishments toward her own goals. (*Martha is ready for rubrics.*)

James, on the other hand, is still in need of external supports. James likes to see his bee in the hive and that he is working toward a goal, but he is not yet internalizing it. He will very soon, so continue to support him in this manner.

What is the feeling when Martha's bee is no longer moved and James and the others are still continuing up the hive? Simply stated, nothing. You may find Martha telling kids "It's OK; I don't care" and that is because she really doesn't care any longer. You can say Martha has moved on to rubrics and you all are going to get to move on very soon as well. Or you may choose not to use a beehive or similar form of behavior modification and do this in language development only. Either way, you are building successes from ant hills, and by the time the child has a mountain of positives, she is ready for the rubrics.

Rules: The Fourth *R*

18. Most likely you will have gotten through all that you wanted to accomplish on the first day of school. You may have 30 minutes left to develop rules with the students, but, if not, then first thing on the second day of school, your opening session will be on rule development.

The students are great at rules. They know them all, but they do not always follow them. When children break rules, they learn from their mistakes, and the adults will need to assist them to regulate so that rule breaking becomes reflective and not purposeful.

Work as a whole group on rule writing. All stakeholders are involved in developing rules for the classroom or for the school. Transition to the rug or large-group circle. You may want to use the smart board for this activity and add technology, as there are many programs offered for writing rules. But beware that you keep all rules clear and concise and when using the programs keep them "your rules, not the ones associated with the program." This means that, often, premade technology programs use negatives. You will want to change these or make your own technology program to keep it positive from beginning to end.

We also want to teach what the rule means before we say it's a rule. For instance, no hitting means to touch nicely or kindly. You may want to model this with the children, so that later on in the day you can say "Look at you, touching kindly and nicely; you know how to use your hands. Hands are not for hitting; they are for exactly what you are doing, Teddy. I am very proud that you know how to touch your friend kindly." We will want to continue this frame of mind and teach the rules before we have to say no hitting. By that time, it's over and done, and the rule is already broken.

Rules should be written with *no* as much as possible. *No* is clear and concise and leaves no room for anyone to interpret anything other than what it says. Here is an example of your rule chart:

Our Classroom Rules
No hitting.
No fighting.
No biting.
Complete your class/center work.
Bring in homework each day.
No speaking when someone else is speaking (or no interrupting).
No calling out.

It is apparent that there is no room for misunderstandings in this rule chart. It is precisely as your children wrote it. They will want to use *no* in their language, as *no* is the language most understood by children, along with *yes* (*rules aid in regulation and create boundaries. Children want and need boundaries to help them learn to regulate. As they begin to self-regulate, they will self-monitor their behavior, as they will have guidelines to follow*).

19. The rule chart may also contain rewards and consequences, and it is suggested that your consequences be ones that come from not paying attention to the negative behavior that was discussed in your readings. If necessary, you may want to include behavioral consequences such as the following:

- *No hitting* would require the hitter learn to work with the child whom he hit. Many times, young children will hit because they do want to be friends but do not know how to accomplish this task.
- *Complete homework* may require the homework be prioritized, so that only those items that need practice are sent home for completion. Homework can be done before or after school if arrangements are made. Many teachers feel this is not at home and they are correct. But it is better for the child to be successful at completion no matter where the work is accomplished.
- *Rewards:* Remember an internal reward is a sense of accomplishment or achievement and comes from one's own actions, as in Martha's case. As the teacher, you are continually noticing these behaviors and commending in a positive and sincere way by stating exactly what the child is doing correctly. An external reward is one that motivates the child from an outside source, such as a treasure box, certificates, awards, or prizes. To help the child move from external to internal rewards, continue to use *The Student Empowerment Program* and the 5Rs.

Rubrics: The Fifth *R*

20. Assuming that you have made the commitment to yourself and the students for the past few days of school, you will find that the students are beginning to assume responsibility for self and others; they are respecting each other, as well as the equipment and physical space of the classroom and school; and they are working within the boundaries of the rules. The adults in the classroom are also following the rules and not taking advantage of their adult status. Respect abounds among all stakeholders when everyone is included in all aspects of the classroom environment. The more you pour on the first 4Rs, the more you will see a culture in the classroom developing into a positive one. It is now time to add the last *R* to your program.

Rubrics will become a common word among all of the objectives and goals in the classroom, from setting the table in the early grades to calculating multiplication and division in the upper grades.

21. Transition into introducing rubrics by playing the rubric song from YouTube titled "Phillip Glass Rubric," found at https://www.youtube.com/watch?v=hStHPRzmSWo. It is your readiness set when introducing a rubric in the classroom. You can use this readiness set as a cue, both visually and auditorily, each time you deliver a new rubric. It will become fun to "wait for the rubric instruction" after part of this is played on the big screen (or smart board).

This YouTube video may also be initially introduced as a reflection exercise to upper-grade students. You may choose to play it and then brainstorm ideas regarding the students' thoughts about it. After the experience, you can tell the children the name of the video, accentuating the word *rubric*. Wait for a response, and then ask open-ended questions, such as "Why do you think it is called rubric?" (Wikipedia states: "Glassworks" is a chamber music work of six movements by Philip Glass. The layering of contrasting timbres is characteristic of the piece as a whole.)

All rubrics must be introduced so that students know what is expected of them. When you begin this song and video on the smart board, it is an engaging brain experience. It is the signal for all children to prepare themselves for a new achievement. It is futuristic in nature and can be an explosive, fun way to start the learning process.

SUMMARY

It is imperative to look at each moment as new. Mistakes will happen, conflicts will exist, social and emotional learning will fluctuate like the tides, and academics may be lackadaisical at times. During all of this, it is important for the teacher to remember what her intention is and how she has committed to making a positive change. It is OK to flow with those tides and to make spur-of-the-moment decisions, but attempt not to become frustrated or stressed.

Take it one step at a time, one moment at a time, and address what needs to be addressed. Learn to allow others to speak. Be a good listener. Learn how to keep the class moving forward while you take time to help a single student. Take the time to teach how to avoid problems, breathing to decompress, and why lifelong learning is important. Every day, assume the responsibility for the care of your students' brains. Reflect, regulate, and create positive rules and follow them consistently, fairly and equally for all. In the end, layer learning through rubrics to create self-dependent, not teacher-dependent, learners.

Index

administrators: internet permission by, 97; open-ended play evaluated by, 49; project time requirements and, 52–53; on teacher facilitation, 58–59; teachers and classrooms judged by, 43; technology requirements by, 96
amygdala, 7
assessments: in consolidation for closure, 100–101, *101*, *102*, *103*; for early childhood learning brain, xiv; evaluations and, 49, 52–53, 68–71, *70*, 82, 89; methods of, 81–83; portfolio assessment as, 82, 88–89; as private or standardized, 28; rubrics and, 79, 81–83, 90–91; stress relieved on, 28

beehive, 17, 119–20
behavior modification: behavior charts as negative, 19–20; for classroom management, 14, 16; parents using, xii, 21; positive tone as, 3; program for, xi–xii; rewards as positive, 118–19
brain-based learning, xi, 2, 7, 21–22
brain development: amygdala in, 7; BRS in, 75; closure and, *36*; dynamic cycles in, 66–67; in first three years, 106; hippocampus in, 3, *15*; learning centers for, 67; lesson design incorporating, 61–62; limbic system and, 11, *15*; medial prefrontal cortex and, 73–74; metacognition and, 66–67; from open-ended play, 51, 75; prefrontal cortex in, 11–12, *15*, 51, 73–74; reflection for higher, 8; SPP in, 75; young child's brain and, 66–67. *See also* early childhood learning brain
brain stimulation reward (BRS), 75
breathing techniques, 5–7, 18, 46
BRS. *See* brain stimulation reward

Campus School, 38
CCSS. *See* Common Core State Standards
classroom activities: early elementary, xi; internet in, 86, *87*, 89, 97; parents in, 115; reflection and, *9*; rituals in, 47, 57; routines in, 9, 47, 116; students and rules of, 16–17; transitions between, 3, 39, 47, 117–18; transition time activities in, 118–19
classroom environment: administrators judging, 43; for cognitive skills, 42; early childhood learning brain and, xiii, 35; ECERS–R, PCMI, SELA Rating Scale for, 44, 46; floor plan for, 43–46, *45*; ideal type of, 44; implementation of secure, 115; with inviting atmosphere, 39; for physical development, 42; short lessons for overcrowded, 43; for social, emotional development, 42; square footage per student in, 43; teacher modeling, 3–4, 20, 28, 39, 46; tour of, 116; video games emulated in, xiv
closure: brain model and, *36*; consolidation for, 65, 75–76, 100–

101, *101*, *102*, *103*; student work needing, 53
cognitive skills: classroom environment for, 42; nature of learner and, xii–xiii, 25–26; from open-ended play, 51, 75; parents collaborating on, 42; play for, 58, *59*; for students, 47; value for, 103
Common Core State Standards (CCSS), 61–66, 76–77, 98
confidence: "M" student story for, 40–41; students developing, 26, 47
conflict resolution, 7–10, 59
consequences, 17–18, 20, 72, 105, 122; parental advice on, *15*, 16
consolidation for closure, 53, 65, 75–76, 100–101, *101*, *102*, *103*
creativity: critical thinking and, 42, 48, 54; early childhood learning brain for, xiii; open-ended play producing, 51–52; students developing, 26
critical thinking, 59, 85, 98; creativity and, 42, 48, 54; early childhood learning brain for, xiii; from reflection, 8, 11, 39

Demonstration of Student Learning (DSL), 73, 85, 98
Dewey, John, 37
Diamond, Marion, 49–50
discipline, 14
DSL. *See* Demonstration of Student Learning

early childhood learning brain: assessments and rubrics for, xiv; classroom environment and, xiii, 35; creativity for, xiii; 5Rs and, xiv; lesson design for, xiii; nature of learner and, xii–xiii; play and, xiii, 49; "process, not product" and, 52; rubrics for, xiv, 80; Student Empowerment Program and, xii; technology and, 93

Early Childhood Learning Standards, 61–63
ECERS–R, PCMI, SELA Rating Scale, 44, 46
educator rating scale, 86–87, *87*
EFT. *See* Emotional Freedom Technique
Emilia, Reggio, 37, 82
Emotional Freedom Technique (EFT), 6
emotional security, *88*; assessments and, 28; breathing technique and, 5, 7; classroom environment for, 42; dramatic play and, *59*; learning from, 1, 11, 35, 42, 55; nature of learner and, xii–xiii; play for observing, 87; prefrontal cortex and, 51; rubrics assessing, 83; rules for, 37; safe environment for, 3, 39–40, 72; special needs adaptions and, 105; for students, 26, 47; of teacher, 3–4; video games and mood swings in, 105, 110
essential question, 73, 85, 98
evaluations: administrators and, 49; criterion for student, 68–69; project approach and, 69–71, *70*; standardized tests and, 82; of teachers, 52–53, 89. *See also* assessments
exploration: definition of, 50; early childhood learning brain for, xiii; Learner's Brain Model and, xiii, 49; planning from, 51, 53, 55, *59*

fairy tale lesson, 94–96, *95*
1st Grade, *8*, *9*, 29, *31*
5Rs, xi–xii; early childhood learning brain and, xiv; implementation of, 114; as reflection, rules, regulation, and rubrics, 46–47; as responsibility, 46–47, 114–16; Student Empowerment Program and, 46
5th Grade, *8*, *9*
4th Grade, *8*, *9*, 30, *32*

gamers. *See* video games
Gardner, Howard, 27–28
goals, 73–74, 122
grade levels, 8, 9, 29–30, 31, 32–33

Head Start, 38–39
hippocampus, 3, *15*

imagery, 5, 7, *9*, 12
implementation, 113–16
independent learners: as self-dependent, xi–xii, 1, 8; students as, 47, 52, 79, 93, 117
informational stage, *36*
instructional delivery, 62, 94, 99–100
internet: administrator permission on, 97; as classroom material, 86, *87*, 89, 97; Skype or FaceTime via, 104; smart boards using, 16, 30, *31–32*, 94, 96–101, *101*, *102*, *121*, 123
iPads, 94, 96–97, 105, 107–8, *109*

kindergarten, *8*, *29*, *32*; learning centers in, 83; music in, *9*; NAEYC required for, 62; NAEYC standards in, 64–65; preparation for, xi; rubric for, *83*, *101*; snack and milk for, 118
KWLH chart, 85, 89, *90*

Leap Frog, 105
Learner's Brain Model, 23, 98–100; gamers and, 72; Leap Frog used in, 105; play and exploration in, xiii, 49; technology with, xiv, 93; video game stages and, 105
learning: active engagement for, 24; auditory input for, 25; as brain-based, 7; emotional security for, 1, 11, 35, 42, 55; goals for, 73; hands-on, 67–68; inviting atmosphere for, 39; from knowledge consolidation, 75–76; mindfulness and imagery for, 5, 12; from "M" story, 40–41; music for, 27–28; pattern seeking for, 75; from peers, 76; prefrontal cortex for, 11–12; prior knowledge for, 73–74; progress and rewards from, 74; project approach for, 67; retention and, 80–81; safe environment for, 3, 39–40, 72; self-dependent, xi–xii, 1, 8; of self-regulation, 14; sense and meaning for, 105; sleep importance in, 26; styles of, xi–xii, 23, 53; technology for, 104
learning centers: for brain development, 67; classrooms with, 44; in prekindergarten and kindergarten, 84; regulation from using, 39, 117; responsibility for, 115
lesson design: after play, 58; assessments and rubrics in, 83; books and computers for, 65; brain development from, 61–62; for early childhood learning brain, xiii; Early Childhood Learning Standards and, 61–63; five stages of, 72–76; gamers and, 72; hands-on learning in, 67–68; NAEYC and, 63–64; nature of learner and, 61; open-ended questions in, 7; outer space example of, 83–89, *84*, *87*, *88*; readiness set, 94–95; sense and meaning created in, 62; smart board in, 97–101, *101*, *102*; standards addressed in, 85, 98; in Student Empowerment Program, 29; teachers and, 61–64; technology incorporated in, 94–95, 104; video games compared with, 77
limbic system, 11, *15*
listening: as encouraged, 24; safe environment from, 3, 39–40, 72; self-regulation and, *15*; skills in, 86, 116, 119; by teachers, 39–40, 86, 116, 119, 123

materials: books and computers as, 65; free-play, 53; internet as, 86, *87*, 89, 97; project approach for, 71
medial prefrontal cortex, 73–74
metacognition, 51, 66–67

mindfulness, 4–7, 12, 18, 46
Montessori, Maria, 11, 37, 49–50, 109, *109*
Mr. Roger's Neighborhood, 108
multiple intelligences, 27–28
music: in kindergarten, *9*; for learning, 27–28; in play, *59*; as signal, 39, 117–18

National Association for the Education of Young Children (NAEYC), 62–65, 71–72, 110–11
nature of learner: cognitive factors in, xii–xiii, 25–26; definition of, 23; gamers and, 72; learning styles for, xii, 23, 53; lesson design and, 61; as social and emotional characteristics, xii–xiii; understanding of, 47–48
negative body language, 19

open-ended free play: administrators evaluating, 49; creativity from, 51–52; definition of, 51; example of, 57–58; LEGO set example of, 53; open-space for, 53; play and, xiii, 49–51, 53–56, *56–57*, 58–59, *59*, 87; sense and meaning from, 51, 75; snack and milk during, 118; Student Empowerment Program and, 54; teacher role during, 54–55, 58–59; time needed for, 52–53; types of, *59*
open-ended questions, 3, 7, 9, 116
open-space school concept, 37–38, 53
outer space example, 84–89, *84*, *87*, *88*

parents: behavior modification used by, xii, 21; in classroom activities, 115; cognitive skills collaboration of, 42; consequences advice for, *15*, 16; play used by, 50; portfolios and, 82; "process, not product" for, 52; projects including, 69, 71; retention noted by, 80–81; rubric data for, 83;

rules including, *33*; technology use and, 107, 110
Peanuts gang, 25
"Phillip Glass Rubric," 123
Piaget, Jean, xiii, 50
planning, *15*, 51, 53, 55, *59*
play: cognitive skills learned in, 58, *59*; early childhood learning brain for, xiii, 49; emotional security observed in, 87; emotions and dramatic, *59*; emotions observed in, 87; exploration and, xiii, 49–51, 53, 55, *59*; as facilitated, 54–55, 58; lesson design and, 58; music in, *59*; open-ended free play as, 49, 51–55, 57–59, *59*, 75, 118; parents using, 50; planning from, 51, 53–55, *59*; rules of, 55; social skills from, 50; types of, 55–56, *56–57*
portfolio assessment, 88–89; parents and, 82. *See also* assessments
positive feedback, 18–19
positive forward-moving charts, 20–21
prefrontal cortex: emotions, planning, skill building, and problem solving developing, 51, 75; learning mode in, 11–12; as medial, 73–74; self-regulation in, *15*
prekindergarten: learning centers in, 83; NAEYC required for, 62; snack and milk for, 118; teaching methods for, xi; Universal Prekindergarten as, 53, 61, 64–65
Preschool Teaching and Learning Standards, 63
prior knowledge: for learning, 73–74; in outer space example, 85
"problems are solved" (PS Land), 7
"process, not product," 52
project approach, 72; administrator requirement on, 52–53; evaluation criteria in, 69–71, *70*; materials accumulated in, 71; nine-step process

in, 67–68; parents included in, 69, 71; stage setting in, 68–69
PS Land. *See* problems are solved
punishment: beehive and, 17, 119–20; as consequences, 122; red light, green light as, 20
Pyramid Learner's Brain Model, *36*

rats and play, 49–50
RBT. *See* Revised Bloom Taxonomy
Reader Rabbit, 106
readiness set, 65, 85, 89, 94–95, 98–99, 123
readiness stage, *36*
red light, green light, 20
reflection: anecdotal records of, 9–10; brain skills from, 8; breathing techniques and, 18, 46; carried over, 11; classroom applications of, *9*; critical thinking from, 8, 11, 39; on fairy tale lesson, 94–96, *95*; first exercise on, 117; in 5Rs, 46; mindfulness for, 46; as ongoing, 9; open-ended questions for, 9; plans and actions connected in, 11; in project approach, 71–72; regulation precursor as, 8; reporting on, 10; as scaffolding to previous, 7–8; self-regulated learning from, 76; value of, 8, *8*; viewpoints accepted in, 10
regulation: first steps on, 116; in 5Rs, 46–47; focus for, 5; learning center use and, 39, 117; from positive feedback, 18; reflection as precursor and, 8; self-dependent learning from, 8; snack sizes and, 118. *See also* self-regulation
resilience, 26
resourcefulness, 26
responsibility: in 5Rs, 46–47, 114–16; for learning centers, 115; rubrics for, 21, 122; rules for, 16, 18; teachers modeling, 46

retention, 80–81
Revised Bloom Taxonomy (RBT), 89
rewards: beehive and, 17, 119–20; learning and, 74; positive behavior, 118–19; rubrics after, 120; rules including, 122; teachers giving verbal, 116
rituals, 47, 57
routines, 9, 47, 116
rubrics: achievement from, 123; for art, *90*; assessments and, 79, 81–83, 90–91; as chart, *84*; definition of, 79; for early childhood learning brain, xiv, 80; educator rating scale in, 86–87, *87*; emotions assessed by, 83; in 5Rs, 46–47; independence with, 47; for kindergarten, *84, 102*; in objectives and goals, 122; parents and data from, 83; "Phillip Glass Rubric" for, 123; project approach and, 72; responsibility and, 21, 122; rewards preparing for, 120; Student Empowerment Program with, 79
rules: behavior modification from, 14, 16; clear definitions of, 121; consequences in, 17, 20, 72, 104, 122; for emotional security, 37; on first or second day, 120; in 5Rs, 46; for learning, 37; new rules added in, 18; parents included in, *33*; for play, 55; as posted, 17; for responsibility, 16, 18; rewards and consequences in, 122; rule chart use in, 119; self-control and self-regulation from, 46; students developing, 16–17, 121; from teacher, 3; technology and, 121

schools: behavior modification for, 14, 16; Campus School and, 38; Head Start and, 38–39; as open-space, 37–38
2nd Grade, *8, 9,* 30, *33*

self-control: from rules, 46; self-regulation versus, 11–12, *15*; Student Empowerment Program for, 1
self-dependent learning, xi–xii, 1, 8
self-regulated learning (SRL), 12
self-regulation: for independent learning, 52; learning strategies for, 14; listening and, *15*; from play, 50; process of, 12; reflection for, 76; regulation as, 5, 8, 18, 39, 46–47, 116–18; rubrics for, 79; from rules, 46; self-control versus, 11–12, *15*; from self-talk, 6, *9*, 12–14; steps for, 12–14, *15*; stress and arousal versus, *15*; Student Empowerment Program for, 1; student evaluations and, 68–69; teachers modeling, 14, 24, 47, 118, 121
self-talk, 6, *9*, 12–14
sense and meaning: for learning, 105; lesson design creating, 62; from open-ended play, 51, 75; stories with, 7
skills addressed, 85, 98
smart boards, 16, 30, *32–33*, 121, 123; teachers and lesson design with, 94, 96–101, *101*, *102*
social skills: from play, 50; rating scale for, 87–88, *88*; students developing, 26
SPP. *See* superior pattern processes
SRL. *See* self-regulated learning
standardized tests, 28, 82, 89
standards: CCSS and, 61–66, 76–77, 98; Early Childhood Learning Standards and, 61–63; lesson plan addressing, 85, 98; of NAEYC, 62–65, 71–72, 109–11; positive outcomes from, 21; Preschool Teaching and Learning Standards as, 63; of school district, 62
Student Empowerment Program: as brain-based learning, xi, 2, 21–22; Diamond research on, 49–50; early childhood learning brain and, xii; 5Rs and, 46; flow chart for, *36*; grade scenarios in, 29–30, *31*, *32–33*; implementation of, 113–14; lesson design in, 29; play and tweaks in, 54; play within, 52; positive forward-moving charts with, 20–21; rubrics in, 79; for self-dependent learning, 1; as stand-alone program, 2; as whole-child program, 21–22
student learning target, 73, 98
students: acceptance and tolerance of, 48; classroom design for, 43–46, *45*; classroom rules developed with, 16–17; closure and work by, 53; cognitive confidence for, 47; creativity developed by, 26; developmental levels of, 62; dispositions developed for, 26; emotional and social confidence for, 26, 47; evaluation criterion for, 68–69; focus learned by, 5; as independent learners, 47, 52, 79, 93, 117; learning from, 76; learning styles of, xi–xii, 23, 53; listening skills for, 39–40, 116, 119, 123; open-ended questions for, 116; Peanuts Gang personalities in, 25; personality survey and circle sharing by, 26–27; play accomplishments of, 51, 53–55, *59*; play for older, 55–56, *56–57*; portfolios and worksheets of, 87–89; positive behavior reward for, 118–19; progress and rewards for, 74; prompting and withdrawal from, 24–25; regulation first steps for, 116; rules created by, 16–17, 121; safe environments for, 3, 39–40, 72; separation anxiety for, 115–16; skills developed by, 26; sleep and learning for, 26; story by "M," 40–41; strengths and weaknesses of, 27; teachers knowing, 24; teachers "read" by, 42, 115; technology use

and, 106–7; transitions for, 3, 39, 47, 117–18; types of, 27; understanding of, 47–48
superior pattern processes (SPP), 75

teachers: with acceptance and tolerance, 48; administrators on, 43, 60; without anger or sarcasm, 25, 46; child brain research for, 66–67; cognitive value by, 103; early elementary classrooms and, xi; emotional security of, 3–4; environment modeled by, 3–4, 20, 28, 39, 46; evaluations and, 52–53, 90; on expectations before event, 118–19; imagery used by, 7, *9*, 88; lesson plan development by, 61–64; listening skills of, 39–40, 86, 116, 119, 123; names and specifics by, 3; open-ended play and role of, 54–55, 58–59; personalities, intelligence, strengths known by, 24; play and lesson plans by, 58; project approach for, 67; prompting and support withdrawal by, 24–25; responsibility modeled by, 46; retention noted by, 80–81; rules from, 3; self-regulation modeled by, 14, 24, 47, 118, 121; smart boards used by, 94, 96–101, *101*, *102*; students observed by, 119; students "reading," 42, 115; technology use and, 106–7; verbal rewards by, 116; young child's brain and, 66
technology: administrative requirements on, 96; digital storytelling as, 104; early childhood learning brain and, xiv, 93; guidelines for, 108–9; handwriting decline from, 105–6; as interactive, differentiated, collaborative, and communicative, 96–97; iPads as, 94, 96–97, 105, 107–8; Leap Frog and Reader Rabbit as, 106; Learner's Brain Model and, xiv, 93; as learning experience, 102; lesson designs incorporating, 94–95, 103; maximum time for, 108; *Mr. Roger's Neighborhood* and, 108; NAEYC guidelines on, 110–11; parents and use of, 107, 110; purpose for, 112; rule creation using, 121; Skype, FaceTime as, 104; smart boards in, 16, 30, *32–33*, 94, 96–101, *101*, *102*, *121*, 123; students and, 106–7; teachers using, 106–7; video games as, 105
3rd Grade, *8*, *9*, 30, *33*
time-out chairs, 19
transitions, 3, 39, 47, 117–18
troubled, 14

Universal Prekindergarten, 53, 61, 64–65

video games: classroom emulating, xiv; five stages of, 72–76; lesson design compared with, 77; mood swings after, 105, 110; as technology, 105

young child's brain, 66–67

About the Authors

Dr. Mario C. Barbiere is a passionate practitioner with a strong theoretical background as a teacher, school administrator at all levels of administration, assistant superintendent, superintendent, professor, and school turnaround specialist. He is committed to closing the achievement gap and providing positive student academic success. He worked at the district and state level for school turnaround while promoting student self-regulation and empowerment. He has authored two books on brain research and lesson design and two books on brain research and instructional delivery, based on his doctoral studies regarding educational neuroscience and practical experience in education.

Jane Wiatr is a 34-year early childhood education veteran, intervention and referral services chairperson, 504 chairperson, and antibullying specialist in New Jersey. Her experiences in prekindergarten Head Start and her many years in the early childhood classroom have served as the foundation for her strong early childhood philosophies. Jane believes in the social, emotional, and cognitive domains of learning through hands-on experiences. Play of all types is highly stressed in Jane's world. Self-regulation and -reflection, as well as nontraditional teaching methods, are her forte, and she has proven this by teaching how to implement positive strategies and techniques to gain results. Jane began the first mainstreaming inclusion program in her district and the first Alternate Route program for prekindergarten through third grade for students at Kean University. Jane is a lifelong learner and continues to build skills by presenting workshops to parents and educators and doing private tutoring.

www.ingramcontent.com/pod-product-compliance
Lightning Source LLC
Chambersburg PA
CBHW070734230426
43665CB00016B/2230